"CAN'T YOU FEEL IT?" RANDI SCREAMED.

Matthew didn't know what she was talking about; he didn't feel anything. But the pounding in the room set up a similar hammering in his chest. He set down the candle and moved to the phone, but as he reached for it, it rose off the table and flew across the room.

Suddenly they both heard a low moaning, as if someone was in great pain. It mushroomed into an ear-splitting wail that shook the windows. Abruptly the candle flickered and all the noise ceased. By the dim light of the street lamps, Matthew watched in horror as Randi grabbed her stomach and screamed as she doubled over.

Matthew ran to her. Her blouse was bloody as he pried away her fingers . . .

*True
Tales
of the
Unknown*

True Tales of the Unknown

Edited by Sharon Jarvis

BANTAM BOOKS
TORONTO • NEW YORK • LONDON • SYDNEY • AUCKLAND

TRUE TALES OF THE UNKNOWN
A Bantam Book / July 1985

ISBN 0-553-24540-6

Published simultaneously in the United States and Canada

Bantam Books are published by Bantam Books, Inc. Its trade-
mark, consisting of the words "Bantam Books" and the por-
trayal of a rooster, is Registered in U.S. Patent and Trademark
Office and in other countries. Marca Registrada. Bantam
Books, Inc., 666 Fifth Avenue, New York, New York 10103.

PRINTED IN THE UNITED STATES OF AMERICA

H   0 9 8 7 6 5 4 3 2 1

Acknowledgments

The following people deserve special appreciation and thanks, for without their research and assistance this book would not exist: Roxanne Salch Kaplan; Joseph Pumilia; Kevin D. Randle; Tom Sciacca.

Also thanks to Dr. Stephen Kaplan of the Parapsychology Institute of America. Those interested in contacting the institute may write directly to P.O. Box 252, Elmhurst, NY 11373. Please include a stamped self-addressed envelope.

Anyone wishing to contact Captain Randle regarding UFOs and other phenomena may write to him at P.O. Box 582, Cedar Rapids, Iowa 52406. Please include a stamped self-addressed envelope.

And thanks to Bill Wallace, who made available his copy of Ingram's long-out-of-print book on the Bell Witch; Gloria Lawrence and Linda Cuda of the Little Falls Public Library; the *Evening Times*, Little Falls, New York; and Joe Kelly of the *Utica Observer-Dispatch*, New York.

And thanks to all of you out there who believe, as we do, that we are not alone. . . .

Introduction

I've always loved good ghost stories. But the true horror of such tales didn't hit me until I realized that some of them actually happened. From that moment on, my fascination with the strange and the bizarre has grown, and I have tried to track down physical proof of the supernatural.

On one case, I searched out a graveyard in upstate New York. The tombstone of a witch killer was said to bear the imprint of the witch's wrath long after the bones of both had turned to dust. I was quite disappointed to find that the gravestone was a monument of varicolored marble, and any one of the colored blotches might be construed as her famous footprint. So much for that witch.

Once I hunted out a particular street that was said to be visited nightly by ghost lights. The people who lived in the tiny town claimed that the lights were the spirits of the dead seeking out their loved ones. I was directed to the end of East Main Street, only to find that Main Street had no East or West and was only three blocks long.

A few more similarly futile efforts ended my search for proof of the supernatural. But I should not have given up my quest so easily. The ghosts, witches, and demons I so eagerly sought were out there waiting for me—and still are. . . .

When I decided to write this book, I already had several wonderful ghost stories in my files—stories that supposedly were true. This time I was determined to search for the truth in the proper way, by creating a network of researchers across the United States, each of whom could provide the necessary legwork to authenticate the stories. These researchers tracked down written records and books in courthouses, churches, newspaper morgues, local libraries, and university libraries. They haunted secondhand bookstores looking for out-of-print volumes and unearthed books, diaries, and long-forgotten tales. They traveled to the actual sites of supernatural occurrences and, whenever possible, interviewed the participants or, in some cases, their descendants.

Thus, many of these tales are reported in the actual words of the participants—victims and witnesses. In the case of "The Corpse That Wouldn't Tell," the story is taken directly from tape-recordings.

The following are seven true stories of supernatural phenomena. Some occurred in the last century, others just a few years ago. Some are quite horrible and frightening, some bizarre and incredible. All are fascinating: the innocent invitation to a demon. The tape-recording of ghostly footsteps. The remarkable clairvoyance of a frontier lawman. These tales are not easily forgotten—and they are only a few of the thousands of true tales of the unknown waiting to be told.

—Sharon Jarvis
Staten Island, N.Y.
November 1983

Contents

The Great American Ghost Story

Even the most talented writer of occult novels would find it difficult to create as horrifying and fantastic a tale of ghosts and hauntings as the true story of the Bell Witch of Tennessee. This famous case is frequently cited in books on the supernatural; however, the following expanded account is taken directly from the testimony of eyewitnesses, most of whom were members of the Bell family.

Do not expect the usual filmy wraith or cackling old hag of popular ghost tales. The Bell Witch was unique. There have been other hauntings that exhibit similar phenomena, but none with such immense power and frequency.

The Bell Witch was not a witch in any sense of the word. Perhaps it was called that because of its feminine voice or because it sometimes appeared in animal form, like a witch's familiar. It was a spirit that possessed amazing powers—powers that would be considered God-given, were they not so incredibly evil. . . .

True Tales of the Unknown

In the early 1800s, Tennessee was considered the "far West" and attracted many settlers from the East. In 1804, the Bell family left North Carolina in a wagon train with all their household goods and their slaves. They settled in western Robertson County, Tennessee, near friends and relatives who had also come from North Carolina. The area they settled in is now known as Adams.

John Bell bought a farm of a thousand acres of the best land on the Red River. According to the slaves, the river bore that name because of an Indian massacre that caused its waters to flow with blood.

Their farm consisted of a large main house and a number of outbuildings. The main house was a double-log building one and a half stories high, with six large rooms and a spacious reception hall. The house was heated by several massive brick fireplaces. An open porch ran the width of the front of the house. It was one of the finest homes in the county. It boasted an excellent orchard, and the front lawn was shaded by immense pear trees reputed to be over a hundred years old.

John Bell was a tall, broad-shouldered, distinguished man with a commanding personality. He was prosperous and influential in the community; his family lacked for nothing. He was a hard worker and a good manager. His wife, Lucy Williams Bell, was a careful, frugal housekeeper. Their children attended the best schools in the settlement and were raised steadfastly in the Christian faith. By 1816, the Bells had nine children. Two were married and living elsewhere in the area; but there were six sons at home, and a daughter, the youngest child, Elizabeth. At first, it did not occur to the Bells that the strange sounds they sometimes heard were other

2

than natural. Therefore, there are no specific dates for their initial encounters with the Witch, or spirit, as it was sometimes called. Richard Williams Bell, a young boy at the time, many years later wrote an account of the affair. It was preserved in *An Authenticated History of the Famous Bell Witch* by M. V. Ingram. Although Ingram expanded Richard's manuscript with some of his own theories, he did not edit Richard's story, and he did add accounts of interviews he conducted with eyewitnesses and their descendants.

According to Richard, the haunting began in 1816 or 1817. There were knockings at the outside doors and scratchings at the outer walls. These were neither frightening nor disturbing. When they continued, John Bell decided that some prankster was responsible and made numerous attempts to apprehend him. But he never discussed the incidents in front of the younger children for fear of frightening them.

In May 1818, events took a strange turn. The six boys occupied a room on the second floor. Elizabeth was in another second-floor room. Mr. and Mrs. Bell had the room below hers.

Seven-year-old Richard and four-year-old Joel were sleeping together this Sunday night when suddenly they heard a sound like that of a rat gnawing on the bed frame. John, Jr., who was twenty-five years old, and Drewry, a few years younger, and with whom he shared a bed, got up, determined to eliminate the noisy rodent. No sooner had they gotten out of bed than the sound stopped. Lighting a candle, the two boys hunted around the bed as a sleepy Richard looked on. Finding nothing, they went back to bed. As soon as their heads touched the pillow, the sound started again. It continued through the night. No matter how often or how thoroughly they searched, they could find no sign of the rat, nor any crevice through which a rat could enter and leave.

The elusive nocturnal rat visited them every night for weeks. The sound seemed to leap from room to room, ceasing only when the whole family was roused. It would commence again when they retired.

But there was worse to come. A vigorous scratching sound, like that of a dog clawing the floor, began to accompany the phantom rat. Yet the Bells could uncover nothing to explain the sounds.

"Nothing was accomplished beyond the increase of our confusion and evil forebodings," Richard wrote years later. "The demonstrations continued to increase, and finally the bed coverings commenced slipping off at the foot of the beds as if gradually drawn by someone, and occasionally a noise like the smacking of lips, then a gulping sound, like someone choking or strangling, while the vicious gnawing at the bedpost continued. And there was no sleep until the noise ceased, which was generally between one and three o'clock in the morning. Some new performance was added nearly every night, and it troubled Elizabeth more than anyone else. Occasionally the sound was like heavy stones falling on the floor, then like chains dragging, and chairs falling over."

The strange persecution of the Bell family then shifted: John Bell, Sr., and Elizabeth were singled out for special attention. Elizabeth is said to have been a "roguish beauty" even at the age of twelve, when the troubles with the Witch began.

Since John and Lucy Bell were at a loss to explain what was happening to their family, the children were

4

sworn to secrecy. The first outside of the family circle to hear of the goings-on was James Johnson, John Bell's closest neighbor and dearest friend.

Johnson and his wife, upon hearing the eerie tale, were bewildered, but eager to help. At the Bells' strange request, they came over to spend a night. The evening began with Bible reading, praying, and the singing of hymns. James Johnson led the devotions.

At the conclusion of Johnson's prayers, the haggard family sat in the firelight, hoping at least for a good night's sleep—even though the Johnsons were curious to see what might happen. The Bell children trustingly watched Mr. Johnson, Bible in hand, his face revealed granitelike by the lanterns. Thus began the end of the Bell family's hopes and dreams.

The company retired. As usual, the gnawing and scratching and knocking began. The Johnsons gasped as their bedcovers flew off. As Mr. Johnson got out of bed to investigate, the Bell family trooped in, and the younger children nodded knowingly as Johnson searched the room. With his wife and the Bells in tow, he searched the rest of the house and discovered the true horror of the visitation.

Chairs and tables had been overturned; lace tablecloths and doilies lay on the floors, mixed in with broken glass and china. All the bedcovers and pillows had been ripped from the beds and strewn to the floor. Papers and books, torn from desks and shelves, littered the floor. It was as if the invisible force had put on a show especially for the pious couple.

But as soon as Johnson and the Bells had lit candles, the disturbances ceased; as they went from room to room, the disturbances stopped, only to begin again in another room. Johnson determinedly followed the sounds, but he found no visible cause.

Then they heard a new sound: it was like someone sucking air through his teeth and smacking his lips.

"In the name of the Lord," James Johnson thundered, "identify yourself!"

The smaller children fearfully awaited the answer. But nothing happened.

They retired again, but no sooner were they in bed than the attacks returned with increasing vigor. Elizabeth cried out. She had felt a stinging slap on her cheek when she resisted the pulling of her covers. Her cheeks were red from the blows of an unseen hand.

An astounded James Johnson, witnessing the girl's assault by an invisible attacker, finally realized the truth.

"It's a spirit!" he cried. "I don't know whom—or what—your supernatural visitor is, but I advise you to tell the settlement. A full-fledged investigation must be conducted."

In the days of the Salem witch trials, the whole Bell clan would have been burned as heretics. But this was a more enlightened era; committees were formed, experiments were undertaken, and a close watch was kept by family and friends.

However, this merely provided more witnesses to the terrible attacks, which continued unabated with Elizabeth as the focus. She was so severely abused by the unknown force that her parents feared for her life.

Finally it was decided that the only solution was to communicate with the invisible being. Neighbors flocked to the Bell home not only to witness the entity's evil demonstrations but to attempt to talk to it—and to get it to talk back. When it rapped on the walls, people rapped back. But that soon became a

6

game, with the ghost rapping out intricate patterns and the neighbors desperately trying to duplicate the sequence.

Eventually someone hit upon an easier method. The neighbors called on the thing to tap on the wall, emit its lip-smacking sounds, or otherwise signal its understanding and answer their questions. Soon the spirit was rapping out the answers to such simple questions as, How many people are present? How many horses are in the barn? How many miles to the next settlement?

It always gave the correct number.

But the invisible creature did not stop there. It began to talk . . .

At first it was only a low, broken, whistling sound, but this soon grew into a faltering whisper. The voice then gained strength. Finally it became strong enough to be heard clearly. The news of this phenomena spread like wildfire. Naturally, the first questions put to the entity concerned its nature and purpose.

"I am a spirit," the voice replied. "I was once very happy but have been disturbed."

Apparently even this effort exhausted the Witch's strength, for no further information about its origin could be obtained. But it did manage to chatter on about numerous other topics. Soon it began to make predictions.

John, Jr., was planning a long trip to North Carolina to settle his father's share of an estate. The night before he left, several neighbors were visiting, evidently hoping that the Witch would put in an appearance. Suddenly all conversation was stilled as the Witch's voice intruded.

"Bad luck," the voice said, cackling. "Bad luck if

you go on the trip. The legal proceedings will not be finished and you will return with nothing."

But John, Jr., was not to be dissuaded. "I don't take orders from an invisible imp!" he said, shaking his fist at his tormentor.

Abruptly the Witch's voice turned silky and cajoling. It announced that an elegant young lady was on her way to visit the county. "You can win her if you stay," the Witch said. "She is very wealthy, owning forty slaves and a fortune."

John, Jr., departed the next morning. It was a six-month journey, and he returned without a penny. Soon after he had left, a young lady who met the Witch's description in every detail arrived. However, she left before John, Jr., returned and he never saw her . . .

The Witch loved to play pranks. Once, when a rabbit was behaving quite strangely, the Witch claimed to have been that rabbit.

The Witch hurled stones and bits of wood at the family and the slaves. Brickbats were thrown at the children as they returned home from school. The children soon learned not to fear this mischief; they marked the sticks with notches and tossed them back. They soon discovered that the sticks thrown at them from the thickets were often the ones they had marked.

At home, the children were greeted by the voice of the Witch recounting everything that had happened during their walk from school. It took credit not only for tossing the sticks and stones but for causing various stumbles along the way.

Richard told of a time when his brother Joel got fed up with the nightly strife and gave the Witch a strong cussing.

"You little rascal!" cried the furious voice. "I'll let you know who you are talking to!" and an invisible hand beat Joel until he almost died.

Although Joel's insults had drawn the Witch's ire, the full force of its wrath still fell on Elizabeth. Every evening at about the time the Witch was due to appear, she would suffer a sort of "spell" or "attack." As the terrified family waited around Elizabeth's prostrate form, nearly a minute might go by between her deep, ragged breaths. She would revive, only to relapse and continue the hideous cycle for nearly three quarters of an hour, after which the spell would pass.

Elizabeth was also slapped, buffeted, and pricked by invisible pins. She was insulted and threatened by the creature. In one case, her shoes seemingly unlaced themselves and flew from her feet as the Witch laughed uproariously.

There was no escaping the Witch. When Elizabeth spent nights at neighboring homes, the Witch followed. But the Bell family was given no respite, for the Witch did not cease its nightly visits to their house. Either the Witch could be in two places at once, or it shuttled rapidly between locations.

Strangely enough, the only member of the tormented Bell family to escape the evil of the Witch was Elizabeth's mother, Lucy, who was an older version of her beautiful daughter. The Witch was, for reasons unknown, Mrs. Bell's fast friend. It always addressed her respectfully, offered helpful household advice, and kept her informed of the affairs of her relatives back in North Carolina.

Some of the Witch's best tricks were performed for Lucy Bell when she was ailing. It sang songs to her, bringing her to tears with verses steeped in pathos. As Lucy's illness worsened, neighbors brought her tempting morsels to stimulate her appetite. So did the Witch.

"Hold out your hands, Luce, and I will give you something," the voice said one day.

Mrs. Bell did so, and from out of mid-air dropped a batch of hazelnuts. Mrs. Bell and her friends glanced up to see if someone had bored a hole in the ceiling, but there was none.

"Say, Luce, why don't you eat the hazelnuts?" the voice asked.

"I cannot crack them," Mrs. Bell replied, astonished.

She had no sooner stopped speaking than they heard a series of small concussions. The nuts were cracked.

The kindness toward Mrs. Bell, however, only highlighted the Witch's cruelty to others. Although the cause of the Witch's aggression was never discovered, it occasionally gave excuses for the things it did.

John, Jr., noticing that the Witch often badgered Elizabeth about her schoolmate sweetheart, Joshua Gardner, asked the Witch why it took such an interest. In reply, it only begged him not to let Elizabeth marry Joshua Gardner.

Gardner was a good prospect for a future husband. He came from a fine family and was a hardy specimen of young manhood. Moreover, he was lively and entertaining and was steadfast during Elizabeth's ordeal. Even when the Witch's voice spewed obscenities to Elizabeth and Joshua in front of their friends, Joshua's love and courage did not abate.

While Joshua sat next to Elizabeth at school, stealing glances at her lovely face marred by the scarlet marks of the Witch's invisible hand, someone else was also watching her: the schoolmaster, Richard Rowell Ptolemy Powell, Jr., a man many years Elizabeth's senior.

Professor Powell was a handsome, elegant man, and some considered him rather a dandy. He cut a striking figure in his high top hat, with his cane, spats, long-tailed coat, and a bit of ruffle at his throat.

Powell had the social and cultural advantage over Elizabeth's young suitors. While bashful boys visited the Bell home on the pretext of wanting to see the Bell sons, Powell hobnobbed with the adults, never missing an opportunity to compliment Mrs. Bell on her bright, lovely daughter. But Powell also suffered the disadvantage of being unable to spend as much time with Elizabeth as her schoolmates could; therefore, he conveyed his admiration to her by means of discreet praise of her schoolwork and by polite conversation when he encountered her outside of school. While Joshua remained steadfast with Elizabeth during the early years of the Witch's attacks, Powell bided his time, waiting for her to grow up.

It is impossible to say how frequently the Witch was present. From written records, it appears to have been fairly constant though cyclical. The Witch generally began pestering the family in the evenings, though it often tormented them during the day as well. In the small hours of the morning it seemed to rest briefly. It never disrupted school. Despite its presence, Elizabeth and the rest of the family were able to carry on with their lives, although they were never able to escape the Witch's shadow during the four years it spent with them.

That shadow fell not only on Elizabeth but on her father John Bell. From the beginning, he too was

11

tormented, but the variations reserved for him often took peculiar forms. Even before the supernatural cause of the early occurrences was recognized, John felt a strange sensation in his mouth—an odd stiffening of his tongue and a feeling as if a stick were pressing against his jaws on each side.

These sensations were fleeting, painless, and infrequent, but they worsened in time. Bell's tongue would swell, making it impossible for him to eat or speak for a day or two. He also suffered facial contortions and tics. As Elizabeth's seizures waned, John's face and mouth problems increased. The Witch, meanwhile, screeched and cursed at "old Jack Bell" and said she would torment him to death. . . .

John Bell had done nothing to merit such horrible affliction. An honest, God-fearing family man, he was bewildered by his notoriety. When people came from hundreds of miles away to see the peculiar situation, John Bell gave them food and lodging. He allowed tents to be set up on his property. He did not charge any fees for his hospitality. It is obvious that the Bell Witch was not a fraud concocted to make money for the family.

Many of these gatherings at the Bell home were occasions for expression of religious faith. The Witch delighted in scriptural controversies and quoted appropriate verses to prove its points. Challenged often, the Witch was always correct. Its comprehensive knowledge of the Bible was mystifying. The Witch is said to have sung hymns, shouted "Amen!" and thumped on the furniture in praise of God, just like any revivalist preacher. Ironically, many members of the community now regarded the Witch as a spirit sent by God to prepare the world for the Second Coming of Christ.

However, eventually religious virtue became too much for the Witch. The entity fell from grace . . . and brought back four "unregenerated" spirits from whatever dimensions it called home. These spirits, apparently not adverse to testing some of the earthly spirits in John Bell's still house, swilled his corn liquor and got very drunk.

Then they roamed through the Bell house, causing a ruckus and stinking up the place with their whiskey-scented breaths. They overturned furniture, pulled quilts off beds, pinched and beat the children, and spat on the slaves.

The four disembodied entities appeared early in the Witch's visitation, but their tour of duty on the earthly plane did not last long. The names these bizarre creatures gave for themselves were Blackdog, Mathematics, Cypocryphy, and Jerusalem. Each had a distinct voice and personality. Blackdog, who spoke in a harsh but feminine voice, was the head of the family. Mathematics and Cypocryphy had delicate, feminine voices. Jerusalem's voice was more like a boy's.

This so-called family manifested in the Bell home as the sounds of drunken carousal. Verbal sparring, filthy language, and blasphemous oaths startled the human visitors, whose eyes followed the voices around the room.

Sometimes the four would launch into a chorus for the entertainment of the crowds and behave quite civilly. This series of concerts marked the end of this phase of the phenomenon. The Witch itself, which apparently was not present when the ghostly family performed, was eventually found to be the cause of it all. It was the author and chief actor in the little

13

drama, changing its voice to impersonate the four other spirits; it had a remarkable talent for imitation.

Once it gave a perfect rendition of the song and prayer that James Johnson had recited the night that John Bell first called him in to help. The performance was flawless according to the witnesses, who claimed they could not distinguish Johnson's words from the Witch's.

Another of the Witch's astonishing abilities was demonstrated for an English visitor who had come to investigate the Witch and ended up staying for several nights. The Witch had a liking for the English visitor and performed many tricks for him, completely convincing the man of its authenticity.

"Now," the Witch announced to him smugly, "I will give you something more to ponder. I will convey a message from you to your family in England."

Prior to this, the Witch had merely reported the goings-on at his home in England, a service the Witch performed for many of its visitors. The truth of its reports had been confirmed by letters from England, but this offer of a two-way communication was a new one.

"Tell them," the Englishman said, "that never since the creation of the world have men seen and heard such marvels as I have seen these past three months!"

"I shall do that," the Witch promised.

Nothing happened immediately, for the Witch seemed to have certain limitations when it came to long-distance travel. Three hours later, the Witch returned. Instead of the Witch's voice, however, they heard the astonished voices of the Englishman's mother and brother. It was as if the Witch had carried a tape-recorder across the Atlantic and recorded their amazement at the Witch's visitation.

When the Englishman returned home, he discovered that the contact with the Witch had been made and that everything it said in the various voices was correct . . .

Other European visitors who witnessed the Witch's performances came to the same conclusion as the Englishman—that only a supernatural being could cause such things. And how did the Bells converse with so many foreigners? It is probable that in many cases the Witch acted as translator, *for it spoke all languages fluently.*

Visitors from every walk of life, from around the world, came to test the Witch, but it was very hard on doubters. A professional detective named Williams appeared at the Bell home one day.

"I've come a long way to settle this weird business," Williams announced.

John, Sr., answered, with a wry, polite smile, "Make yourself to home."

Williams hung up his hat and sat down. "I don't believe in the supernatural—it's all just trickery!" he said.

After suffering a beating at the invisible hands of the Witch, the detective gladly departed at daybreak.

Even Andrew Jackson, an old friend of John Bell, Jr.'s, stopped to see the famous Witch. According to local legend, Jackson did have a run-in with the Witch, but Jackson's diary, although it does document the visit, contains no mention of any supernatural occurrence.

However, Elizabeth Bell asserts that invisible restraints held back a team of horses pulling Jackson's wagon and that the Witch beat some of his men.

15

Perhaps Jackson, predicting that he would one day be famous, did not want such outrageous occurrences recorded in his diary.

By now the ills and abuses inflicted on John, Sr., had begun to take their toll. His health began to decline as the fourth year of the Witch's reign drew to a close. His despair can only be imagined as he lay in bed, his face horribly distorted and twitching, the Witch's murderous threats ringing in his ears. Periodically these spells subsided and he was able to attend to his farm. But, toward the end, the bad spells came more frequently. John Bell was no longer the imposing figure he once had been. He had lost weight and most of his hair. His sons had inherited the imposing Bell figure and looks, which only reminded him of the way he once had been.

After one particularly cruel experience with the Witch, he broke down in front of John, Jr. "Oh, my son," he said, weeping, "I cannot much longer survive the persecution of this terrible thing. It is killing me by slow torture, and I feel that the end is nigh."

At that point he took to bed and never left the house again. Convinced that his time had come, John Bell underwent a gradual decline.

He was able to move about the house to some extent, however; and habitually roused the family each morning. But on the morning of December 19, his wife found him apparently sound asleep. She began preparing breakfast while some of the boys began their chores. When they noticed that he was sleeping unnaturally soundly, they attempted to rouse him, but could not. John, Jr., went to fetch some prescribed medicine from a cupboard, but found the medicine bottle missing. In its place was an unfamiliar bottle containing a smoky brown liquid.

16

Later, one of the neighbors examined the bottle. "I think this is poison," he said angrily, waving the mysterious bottle in the air. "The damned Witch did this!"

He was answered by a disembodied voice crying gleefully, "He will never get up. He will never get up. I did it!"

John Bell never regained consciousness. As he lay dying, the Witch hurtled unseen around the room, shouting and singing vulgar songs. Bell died the next morning. The Witch promised to attend the funeral.

At the graveside, the people of the community waited for the Witch to keep its promise. As dirt was being shoveled into the grave, a wild, familiar voice suddenly began singing, "Row me up some brandy, oh, row, row, row. Row me up some brandy, oh, row me up some more."

After John Bell's funeral, the Witch's activities diminished somewhat, but it still objected to Elizabeth's relationship with Joshua Gardner. Elizabeth, filled with forebodings, feared the consequences should she defy the Witch by marrying against its wishes. Her father's terrible persecution and death were fresh in her mind. Should she wed Joshua? Elizabeth was torn with indecision. Finally, she broke off with him, and he left town.

The Witch then let up on Elizabeth and became quite friendly. As soon as Joshua Gardner withdrew from Elizabeth's life, Richard Powell, her former teacher, began to court her. He was prominent in public affairs, elegant and handsome as always. That he had bided his time over the years until he could openly court Elizabeth stood him in good stead. He spent the next four years winning her hand and

17

replacing Joshua in her affections. Finally they married and by all accounts lived happily until Powell's death seventeen years later.

Before Elizabeth died in 1890, at the age of eighty-six, she told her life story to Dr. Charles Bailey Bell, a great-grandson of John Bell, Jr. Dr. Bell is the author of *The Bell Witch, a Mysterious Spirit*. Published in 1934, the book sheds more light on the mystery, though it does not solve it. It also provides an account, handed down through the family, of John, Jr.'s conversations with the Witch. John, Jr., tended to argue with the Witch; he even taunted it, calling it a coward for tormenting Elizabeth, and dared it to attack him instead. The Witch declined.

Apparently, after his father's death, John, Jr., was still arguing with the Witch, which told John that his father was beyond the reach of all except the Almighty.

"But I could easily have deceived you if I wanted," the Witch said, "by mimicking your father's voice to make it seem as though he were still here."

John, who was trudging through the snow, was in no mood for the evil spirit's boasting. "Begone," he told it. "Leave me alone."

The Witch continued to torment him. "Look at the snow-covered earth," it commanded.

At the spot indicated, footprints appeared, as though an invisible man were walking alongside John, Jr.

"Why don't you see if your father's boots fit the tracks?" the Witch suggested.

"I think not," John declined. "I am well aware of your many talents."

"You need not have worried," the Witch said. "The dead do not return."

18

Soon afterwards, as the family sat before the fire, they heard a rumbling sound from the chimney. It heralded a bizarre apparition that rolled down the chimney and out into the room. Whatever it was, it looked like a black sphere or cannonball and it burst in a puff of smoke.

Then the Witch spoke: "I am going away and will be gone seven years. Goodbye to you all."

The family was stunned. Then a great sense of relief washed over them. But the next seven years were filled with dread as they waited.

By the time seven years had passed, the family had for the most part dispersed. Only Mrs. Bell, Richard, and Joel lived at the old homestead. It was in February or March 1828 that Richard, age seventeen, was awakened. He opened his eyes and stared sleepily into the darkness. Something outside scratched briskly on the weatherboarding. Richard's heart sank and he was filled with despair. The sound came into the room, through the wall, and became a scratching on his bedpost. Suddenly his bedcovers flew off.

Richard fought the invisible Witch for the covers into the small hours of the morning. The next day he said nothing, but Joel and his mother noticed his haggard appearance. They could guess the cause of his sleepless night. Everyone remembered the Witch's promise to return.

During another nightly tussle with the Witch, Richard heard a noise in the other bedroom where Joel slept near his mother's bed. A few moments later, they both hurried into Richard's room and made a pact to tell no one about the return of the Witch.

But the Witch had already visited John Bell, Jr. Its voice had sprung suddenly from the shadows of

19

the room as John sat reading. John put down his book, his jaws clenched with suppressed anger.

"Hello, John," said the familiar voice. "I am in hopes you will not be as angry at me on this visit as you were on my last. . . . I have been in the West Indies for seven years and—"

"Wherever you have been, your proper place is in Hell. You should go there and stay."

The spirit was not daunted. It continued to claim that the family's suffering were not in vain. But it did not explain why this was so, only hinting at some vaster plan and saying that it was all for the best.

The Witch also told John, Jr., that there were spirits millions of years old that had never been incarnated. Presumably, the Witch itself was one of these. When asked why God would permit it to trouble the Bells, it was again evasive, saying that the mere tale of its existence would seem incredible to the world.

The Witch then drifted off into a sermon, railing against so-called preachers who denied the existence of heaven and hell. It urged a religious revival. Napoleon, it said, had suffered defeat because he had not taken God into account, and if Rome had heeded the teachings of Christ it would not have fallen.

The message was as Christian as any ever preached in Robertson County. Satan, it said, was the director of fallen spirits and will eventually be punished. But it admitted that it did not know all things and advised mankind to study the Bible for answers.

Surprisingly, it then interjected a prophecy of a coming civil war in which the slaves would be freed and the South would lose. This came to pass thirty-three years later.

The next night, the Witch again interrupted

John while he was reading. He was looking over a map depicting the Battle of New Orleans, in which he had fought.

"There will always be wars," the Witch said. "There are times when it is best to cease quarreling and just fight it out."

John snorted in reply and resumed his reading. The following evening, the Witch predicted a war that would involve almost the entire world. It would come at a time when the United States would be one of the greatest nations. But the country would suffer morally, financially, and spiritually, it warned, and a complete spiritual adjustment would be needed to hasten the recovery. Beyond that time, it predicted another "great upheaval" and a great social change. Once again, only true spirituality would be the balm.

"Worlds much larger than Earth had been incinerated in a moment," the Witch warned. "A similar fate awaits you. This is not such a prophecy as is found in the Bible regarding the world's end; it is merely to be expected from past observations of mankind."

Finally, the Witch left a prophecy for the United States that was to be handed down in the Bell family. There would be a great and unavoidable calamity— one that was not to be revealed to the world until some time after the catastrophe had occurred.

John Bell, Jr., kept the Witch's final prophecy a secret for years. Eventually he told his son. No one else had ever heard his story of the Witch's final visitation. And then he revealed the Witch's prediction. . . .

On a certain named date in the future, the Witch would return. By then the United States would have "reached a stage in its history when spiritual conditions must improve, when people must acknowledge their obligations and recognize they have a spirit."

On that day there would be a great calamity, and the Witch would be there, making itself known to a Bell descendant, but to help, not to harass. Dr. Charles Bailey Bell, having received the prophecy from his father, the son of John, Jr., was certain that *he* was the Bell to whom the Witch was to appear. He planned to deliver the Witch's message to the world in that "year of the great catastrophe—1935."

Charles had decided that the United States would be the focus of the great calamity. He waited expectantly for 1935 and followed all the events of that year with great anticipation. In 1935, humorist Will Rogers died in a plane crash. United States Senator Huey Long was assassinated. Two hundred tornadoes killed seventy people nationwide. The Great Depression continued unabated. But there was no calamity to fulfill the Witch's prediction.

However, there was one event in 1935 that did lead to a devastating conclusion: Hitler rejected the Versailles Treaty and took a major step toward World War Two. Was this the great catastrophe? And where was the Bell Witch?

There is no record of the Witch's ever appearing to Dr. Bell. The entire prophecy, which he had been given to pass on, has been lost.

The true nature of the Bell Witch—or "spirit," as John Bell, Sr., preferred to call it—remains a matter of dispute. What was the Bell Witch? Many thought it was a spirit from Hell—and not without reason. Some thought it was a sort of "familiar," belonging to a local "witch-woman" named Kate Batts. The Witch itself once claimed this to be the case, but it changed its tune later. John Bell, Sr., did not believe the Witch had anything to do with Kate Batts. However, in some accounts the Witch is addressed as "Kate."

On another occasion it claimed to be the restless spirit of a person whose grave had been disturbed. Another time it claimed to be an Indian ghost. In its final appearance, it claimed to be millions of years old.

John, Jr., accused it of being a "demon spirit." Richard concluded that it was a "fiend of a hellish nature." Perhaps the Witch's own description of its identity is the most accurate: "I am a spirit. I was once very happy but have been disturbed."

There is no evidence to believe that the Witch itself knew what it was. Its various self-identifications indicate that it was casting about for an identity to latch on to, finally settling on the idea that it was an eons-old discarnate entity.

However, the fact that it did not keep its word to return a century later, though it supposedly had been in existence for eons, is highly suspicious. From what is known of its personality, the Witch would have loved to perform before the microphones and cameras of the twentieth-century media.

Was the Bell Witch a fraud? Even at the time, some people refused to believe that a supernatural being was the cause of the phenomena. They thought that Elizabeth was tricking them.

Tests were done, but no fraud was ever uncovered. It is hard to imagine any reason for a man like John Bell to permit crowds of curious visitors to eat him nearly out of house and home. Nor is it likely that John Bell—or any member of the Bell family—would have gone through such a hellish experience just to gain fame.

But an interesting theory, advanced by Representative Eugene Davidson of Adams, Tennessee—and by J. N. Hockenheimer, in a thesis at the University of Mississippi—suggests that although the Bells were innocent, someone else was indeed responsible for creating the Bell Witch: Richard Powell, the future husband of Elizabeth Bell.

Davidson has carefully researched the case and bases his theory entirely on documented evidence, which is sometimes at variance with the stories handed down through the generations. Based on his findings, he thinks Powell was the Bell Witch, and that it was all trickery and nothing supernatural.

Although the traditional Bell Witch legends do not mention it, Powell was familiar with the Bell family before the Witch appeared and was, in fact, invited to the community by John Bell, Jr. Although Powell claimed to be a bachelor, he actually had a wife in Williamson County. Even more remarkable, at the time the Witch first appeared, *Powell was living in the Bell house as a boarder*. (Davidson says he was given this information by descendants of Elizabeth Bell.) There is information, also, that Powell had studied not only the occult but ventriloquism.

"Powell had a very pleasant personality," Representative Davidson said. "He was the type of fellow to whom you'd tell something intimate that you wouldn't tell anyone else. He roamed around and he had the ear of everyone. This could have played a part in the story, as far as how things would be spurted out [by the Witch] about different individuals that someone else didn't know was going on."

Based on the information he recovered from official archives and family histories, Davidson believes the Witch never "appeared" when Powell was not present. Naturally, there are gaps in the documentation, and this theory, while interesting, does not explain how Powell could have caused people to believe they were being beaten by an invisible being, or how he could have read minds, repeated sermons word for word in the preacher's voice, caused footprints to appear in the snow, and so on. A man who could accomplish all this by trickery would be a very remarkable character, and Powell's diary, if it could be found, might prove fascinating. That vital document has been traced from Elizabeth, who possessed it at the time of her death, to North Carolina, where the trail comes to a mysterious end.

So, the question remains—what was the Bell Witch? Or—what *is* the Bell Witch?

Lucy Bell died in 1828, shortly after the Witch returned. The house was left deserted when the property was divided. Apparently no one wanted to live in a house filled with terrible memories or to tempt the Witch to return. For some years afterwards, it was used only as a storehouse, then it was dismantled and moved to a new location.

In the 1850s, Dr. Henry Sugg, who had been a child during the Witch's heyday, visited a patient in the rebuilt Bell house. The sick man told the doctor about various strange events and sounds that had been occurring, but the doctor only laughed. Even as he was laughing, he could hear the rattling of glass bottles in his medical bag. This was followed by the explosive sound of the corks blowing out. However, when he opened the bag, he found it untouched, its contents completely intact.

Dr. Sugg hastily improvised some rational explanation, but while he was speaking the explosive sounds occurred once more, even louder. Again Dr. Sugg opened his bag—again, nothing in it had been disturbed. He could find no explanation for the mystery, but found instead an excuse to leave.

Since that time, whenever anything unusual or odd happens in or around Adams, people often say, "The Witch probably did it," by way of explanation. And, of course, odd things continue to happen. . . .

At the turn of the century, a Judge Turner built his home on a section of the Bell land. A few years ago, before this house was torn down, Bell relatives from Massachusetts came to take photos of it for their family album. One of the photos shows an unidentified member of the party. At the corner of the house stands a red-haired girl holding a baby. Not only is she not one of the relatives, but there was no one standing there when the picture was taken. Who is she? Some lesser ghost basking in the Bell Witch's publicity?

There are still Bells living in Tennessee, and although they are divided in their opinion of the famous Bell Witch, they haven't escaped it entirely. Carney Bell of Springfield is one of the few family members who takes the story of the Witch seriously.

"Most of the others," he said, "take it with a grain of salt. But certain things have happened to me that lead me to suspect that the Witch, or some part of it, still lingers."

Sixteen years ago, Carney Bell's mother woke him with an early-morning phone call. Something had happened, but she wouldn't tell him what. Puzzled, he went down the street to her home, where she met him at the door.

"I want you to look through this house and check all the doors and windows," she ordered. "Because if nobody has gotten out of the house, then there's somebody in the house!"

Carney found all the doors and windows secure, so if there had been an intruder, he was still in there. Carney began a thorough search of the house.

The reason for his mother's odd behavior became evident when he reached the butler's pantry. It was an amazing sight. The doors of the built-in china closet were flung wide. The china was scattered across the floor. It was as if someone had angrily raked all the china out of the cabinet.

Carney Bell saves the best part of the story for last. "None of the china, you see, was broken. It was all good as new. There wasn't even a chip."

Then, about eight years ago, Carney had another run-in with the Witch, which had claimed to take the form of animals, usually a rabbit.

Carney Bell and his four sons were rabbit hunting on what had been part of the old Bell farm. Spotting a rabbit creeping through the brush, Carney fired.

The rabbit went rolling, as though it had been hit, then suddenly recovered and ran up a hill. Carney and his sons followed it into a honeysuckle thicket but found no trace of the animal.

Winded from the chase, they sat down to rest against the headstones of a small, abandoned cemetery overgrown with honeysuckle. The inscriptions in the stones were nearly illegible.

"Dad, look at this marker," one of the boys pointed out.

"What's wrong with it?" Carney asked. Then he looked closer and saw that it was the grave of his great-great-great-grandfather, Joel Egbert Bell, whom the Witch had spanked for cussing! Carney had been trying to locate that grave for years.

Several years later Carney went back to what is

left of the old Bell farm and gathered up the stones of the fireplace. He took them home and built them into his own fireplace. When a good fire is going, he says, he looks into the dancing flames, watching the weird figures they make, and is glad that the Witch hasn't taken more of an interest in him and his family.

He wonders what he would do if a ghostly voice suddenly piped up. . . .

The Man No Man
Could Kill

"Texas" John Slaughter was one of the greatest heroes of the Old West. Walt Disney, in his Sunday-night program back in the 1960s, portrayed this celebrated sheriff as a tall, handsome he-man who fearlessly apprehended desperadoes. Only the last part was true. Slaughter, who stood a mere five foot six, was known as "the man no man could kill."

The reason for Slaughter's uncanny luck and charmed life lay mostly in the fact that he honestly believed he would win any showdown. He faced bushwhackers, killers, and thieves with his badge as a target, not as a shield. He was not afraid to look death in the face because, he claimed, his protection came from a source not of this earth. . . .

An icy finger tapped at the base of John Slaughter's spine. His teeth clamped tightly on his cigar, and his eyes darted to the left and right, searching.

Slaughter's change of expression went unnoticed by the cowhands who rode with him.

The feeling dissipated as quickly as it had come, but Slaughter's sense of impending danger remained. Trouble lurked ahead on the trail—of that Slaughter was certain. His "guardian angel," as he called it, was never wrong. This unseen spirit warned him every time he approached a life-threatening situation.

The warnings were different each time. Sometimes it was a sudden, inexplicable shift of his thoughts. At other times it was an almost physical presence and had a whispered voice. He had learned to heed both, and so had survived the Civil War.

Now Slaughter's gaze rose to the herd of cattle he and his crew were driving north toward the Texas pan-handle. Within a few days they would be on the range of rancher John Chisholm. Suddenly a thin finger of dust rose over the hogback. A moment later, ten men rode into view.

Slaughter watched the riders angle down the slope, riding directly for his position.

They know whose herd this is, he thought. And they know me by sight.

The thought gave him little comfort as the leader reined to a halt before Slaughter's mount. Slaughter recognized him instantly—Barney Gallagher, also known as Curly Bill Gallagher, a Texas rustler and notorious two-gun killer.

Fortunately, Slaughter's men already had their guns trained on the newcomers.

"'Bout a hundred of them cows look like lost stock of mine," the man claimed. "I want 'em cut out of the herd."

Slaughter didn't reply.

"Maybe you heard of me? I'm Curley Bill Gallagher. I usually take what's mine."

Slaughter's right hand dropped and his wrist

flicked. In the batting of an eye, he snapped his .44 from its holster and pointed it at the rustler's face.

"Yep, I heard of you. I'm not impressed. Git!"

Gallagher's eyes met Slaughter's cold gaze. Scowling, he jerked his horse around and called back as he rode away, "Damn you, Slaughter! This ain't the last you've heard of me!"

Slaughter eased his gun back into its holster. For the moment, the danger had passed, and his guardian angel's warning had saved him and his cattle. But he knew Curly Bill would be waiting for him down the trail.

Weeks later, as Slaughter and his trail crew bedded down the herd for the night near Fort Sumner, New Mexico, Gallagher rode out of the evening dusk and told a cowhand, "You tell that little bastard up front I'm here to kill him."

As the cowhand rode off to deliver the message, Gallagher slipped a sawed-off shotgun from his saddle holster and cocked it. He watched Slaughter turn and start riding toward him. Gallagher grinned wickedly as he spurred his own mount forward. Slaughter was a fool—both his hands were on his reins, nowhere near the .44 strapped to his waist.

Certain of victory, Gallagher raised his shotgun.

A pistol suddenly appeared in John Slaughter's hand. A single shot slammed into Gallagher's chest. He slumped and fell to the ground, dead.

Impassively, Slaughter drew his mount to a halt and glanced at his would-be killer. Once again, his guardian angel had warned him. Since meeting Gallagher weeks ago, a mysterious voice had told him to carry his pistol on his saddle horn when he rode, rather than in its holster.

To Slaughter, the incident meant little. But to

those who watched, and to those who later heard of Gallagher's death, it was the birth of a legend—John Slaughter, gunfighter.

John Slaughter was born on October 2, 1841, shortly before his family settled in eastern Texas. When the Civil War broke out, John and his brothers served in the Confederate. When Slaughter was discharged, he joined the Texas Rangers.

It was with them that Slaughter got his first taste of law enforcement and Indian fighting, both of which would serve him well in later years. However, life with the Texas Rangers was not what he had envisioned for himself. Establishing a ranch near those of his brothers, Slaughter was soon driving herds north along the then-new cattle trails.

During his stay in Texas, Slaughter made and lost two fortunes in the cattle business. In 1877 he went to Arizona—with his reputation as a gunfighter preceding him.

He settled in Cochise County, a large rectangle of rugged land bordering Mexico and New Mexico. There he purchased the sprawling San Bernardino Ranch and once more entered the lucrative cattle business.

As John Slaughter's reputation grew, forty-five miles to the northwest another reputation was growing, not of a man but of a town—Tombstone.

Originally a mining camp, Tombstone was now a boom town as miners and cattlemen brought it to a wild, flourishing life.

Whiskey flowed where water didn't. In 1882, Tombstone had seventeen gaming saloons on one block of its main street. Whiskey and gambling—a deadly combination. Fist- and gunfights were the standard fare of the day.

Rustlers, killers, stagecoach robbers—Tombstone drew them all. The law-abiding citizens found help from the famous Dodge City lawman Wyatt Earp and his brothers and their friend Doc Holliday.

While others had praise for the Earps, to Slaughter they were "tinhorn gamblers," no better than those they had been hired to clean out of Tombstone. The Earps knew how Slaughter disliked them and gave him plenty of room when he and his family rode into town. But the gunslinging Doc Holliday made no secret of his hatred for Slaughter.

With Holliday constantly on his mind, Slaughter once again felt the presence of his guardian angel. So he wasn't very surprised when his wife, Viola, had a premonition of danger one night.

Slaughter and Viola had just left the home of a friend and were walking to their carriage. "John, I don't think we should go home this evening," she said. "It's late."

Slaughter shook his head. "I say, I say, I say, Viola. There's nothing to worry about."

Viola smiled. Many people mistook the three "I says" that John began almost every conversation with as a stutter. But it was just a quirk.

"But I feel that we're in danger," Viola insisted.

Slaughter respected and loved his young wife, but he didn't put much faith in anyone else's premonitions. He trusted only the guardian angel that spoke to him. So he helped his wife into the rig, then slid in beside her and took the reins. As they headed home along the Charleston Road, they talked about their children and watched the moon rise.

While Viola's gaze searched the heavens, Slaughter's hand slipped beneath his coat. His guardian

33

angel had finally spoken, and how his gun was in his hand.

"John"—Viola cocked her head to one side—"listen. It sounds like a running horse coming up the road behind us."

"That's exactly what it is," he replied, although he made no attempt to glance behind the wagon.

Viola did, however. "I can't see anybody behind us."

"They ain't on the road. Listen," he answered.

The sound of hooves now came from the east of the carriage. She could hear them in the distance as they moved past the rig and disappeared ahead of them to the south.

Slaughter clucked to the horse, urging it faster down the road. Still keeping his gun beneath his coat, he cocked the hammer, ready for action.

"I hear the horse again," Viola said as they rounded a curve. "It's behind us again."

Slaughter heard it too. Near, he thought. He was probably hiding in that brush we just passed.

The sound of hooves grew closer. Suddenly there was a rider beside them. The warm musky scent of horse sweat filled the air. The rider had worked his mount hard.

Without moving his head, Slaughter shifted his eyes to the side. He knew that horse—and its well-dressed rider.

Abruptly the rider snorted as though in disgust, wheeled his mount around, and spurred it back into the night. Slaughter silently released a long-held breath.

"John, that man had a gun in his hand," Viola said, grasping his arm. "I saw the moonlight glint on the barrel!"

Slaughter chuckled as he raised his hand to show her the Colt he had placed in his lap earlier. He had no doubt that Doc Holliday had followed them with the intention of killing him. However, the "king of the gamblers" hadn't reckoned on meeting up with a guardian angel.

That was the last Slaughter saw of Doc Holliday and the Earps, who fled to Colorado after the infamous gunfight at Tombstone's O.K. Corral.

But the night when Holliday approached the Slaughter carriage was to be replayed, although with a different man set on killing John Slaughter. The man's name was Ike Clanton, head of the Clanton clan.

Although Slaughter was friendly with several members of the Clanton family, he had never liked Ike. The first time the two had met, Slaughter had found Ike on the San Bernardino range, trying to steal his cattle. After heated words, Clanton found himself staring down the barrel of Slaughter's .44. He had ridden off the San Bernardino, vowing to one day kill the no-nonsense rancher.

It was on a buggy drive home with his wife after a shopping trip to Tombstone that John Slaughter once again was warned of impending danger.

"Take the reins awhile, Viola," Slaughter said, passing them to her. "I want my gun in my hand."

Minutes later they heard the sound of hooves. A horseman drew abreast of the carriage, his six-shooter gleaming in the moonlight. The same silvery rays illuminated the barrel of Slaughter's cocked pistol.

Ike Clanton gave wife, husband, and primed weapon but a glance, then slowly dropped his gunhand to his side and rode by without saying a word. . . .

In 1886 Slaughter served with the army. The following year, Tombstone's booming period passed, and Slaughter was elected sheriff. Seeing the opportunity to put an end to the lawlessness in Cochise County, Slaughter pinned on his badge, and the expression "shoot first and ask questions later" was coined.

From his very first case, that of a horse thief, the reputation of this small, quiet man began to spread across the territory—also, the word that this was a lawman whom no man could kill.

All of Tombstone was aware of the horse theft by the time word of the crime reached the sheriff's office. Slaughter felt the tension in the air as he looked up and down the street. The eyes of the town were on him, watching every move.

With a pistol on his hip and a sawed-off shotgun in hand, Slaughter unhitched his horse and swung into the saddle.

"Sheriff, wait up!" deputy Burt Alvord called out. "I'll get my horse and come with you."

Slaughter reined the gray around. The deputy was awkwardly trying to strap on his gunbelt as he crossed the wide street.

"I say, I say, I say, Burt, only one horse was taken. One horse means there's just one thief. Stay here and keep an eye on the town. I'll handle the thief."

Slaughter headed out of town, leaving his deputy and the town staring after him.

Alvord shook his head as he turned back to the office. John Slaughter was a tough little cuss, but he wasn't that tough. A bullet could kill him. Riding off alone like that only made it that much easier for a bullet to find its mark.

Most of the people in Tombstone agreed with Alvord. Heavy bets were placed by the local gamblers. Slaughter's reputation as a fighter was well known, but he had ridden out alone, and lone-wolf lawmen did not last long in the Arizona Territory.

Twenty-four hours passed. Then suddenly a shout went up in front of the Crystal Palace. All heads turned to see the distant rider.

It was Slaughter. Behind his gray, he led the stolen roan. Without a word, Slaughter rode to the sheriff's office, dismounted, and tossed the roan's reins to Alvord.

"Take it to its owner," was all he said before going into the office and closing the door.

Burt Alvord shook his head, turned to the crowd who had gathered, and said, "You'll get more out of a cactus than you will him."

Deputy Lucero grinned from ear to ear. "Now maybe we'll have less horse stealing around these parts!"

Inside, John Slaughter listened to the murmurs that ran through the crowd at Lucero's pronouncement. Apparently his entrance into Tombstone had been more dramatic than he had realized. His silence and that empty saddle showed clearly that law had come to Cochise County.

Of course, leaving the horse thief facedown in the sand hadn't been calculated by Slaughter; it was just a matter of business, part of a day's work. After all, when an outlaw tried to draw on a sheriff, the sheriff simply beat him to the draw, then left him for the buzzards.

Too, having a guardian angel at one's shoulder always helped.

When Slaughter's deputies found the thief's body in a canyon several days later, Slaughter's reputation grew. The people of Tombstone now had actual proof of their new sheriff's prowess with guns.

Tombstone got to know Slaughter as it had never known the sheriffs before him. When the people heard his soft-spoken voice, they listened. Better his "I say, I say, I say" than the bark of his pearl-handled .45 Colt or the explosion of his double-barreled shotgun.

Though Slaughter was not a public man, he made no attempt to conceal himself from Tombstone's residents. He had certain habits and ways of doing things and didn't care who knew it. He always rose before sunup. He always carried his money either in a money belt or in a canteen. He always sat in the same chair at mealtimes.

Such set patterns might have been dangerous for most lawmen, especially those with men vowing to kill them. And there were dozens of outlaws bragging they would someday kill the sheriff who claimed no man could kill him.

But, as set in his ways as Slaughter appeared, he also obeyed the instructions of his guardian angel. And those instructions were just enough to throw off anyone who was keeping an eye on him. One morning he might prepare to ride off on his favorite gray, then suddenly jerk the saddle from the horse's back and toss it onto another horse. Perhaps he had discussed traveling north to Bowie all morning, yet when it was time to depart, he would abruptly wheel his mount around and ride south for Bisbee. He might be riding along a well-traveled road and suddenly rein his horse onto a side road for no apparent reason.

His behavior wove a cloak of mystery about him and made him totally unpredictable to friends and enemies alike. When asked about his impulsive changes, he would roll his cigar to the side of his mouth, shrug, and say that his guardian angel had whispered to him.

Slaughter's faith in the guardian angel made him so confident that once he even took his family with him and Deputy Burt Alvord to Chifton, Arizona, to pick up a man named Jose Lopez, who was wanted for murder. Slaughter had heard that Lopez was holed up in a cabin near Chifton.

Leaving his wife, his son Willie, and Deputy Alvord at the home of friends near Chifton, Slaughter rode out to capture Lopez by himself.

"I wouldn't worry about John none," Alvord reassured Viola and Willie as they watched Slaughter ride away.

Two hours later, John came riding back into town with a handcuffed Lopez. Neither Slaughter nor Lopez bore a mark to indicate that the capture had been anything but peaceful. When Alvord asked his boss how it had gone, Slaughter said, "I say, I say, I say, I got him right here, don't I?"

Slaughter loaded Lopez into his buggy, along with Viola, Willie, and Deputy Alvord, and headed west. When they reached Willcox, Slaughter decided to stop for a rest at a combination general store and saloon. Taking the still-handcuffed Lopez to the rear of the establishment, Slaughter left his prisoner under the guard of his deputy, then rejoined his wife and son out front.

As they passed the time of day with the store's

patrons, Viola noticed a sudden tension come to her husband's jaw as he clamped down on his cigar. She knew his guardian angel was talking to him.

Without a word, Slaughter casually strolled to the back of the store. Alvord stood at the bar, downing his second beer, engrossed in conversation with the bartender.

Slaughter's gaze shifted to the back of the room. Three Mexicans were speaking to Lopez in rapid-fire Spanish. Noticing the cold stare of Tombstone's sheriff, the three hastened from the store. Slaughter had no doubt that the three of them would have tried to make a break with their friend if he hadn't entered when he did.

Reminding Alvord that he had been left to guard Lopez, not to drink the saloon dry, Slaughter returned to his family and announced that they would spend the night in Willcox, then return to Tombstone the next morning.

It was hours before dawn when John gently shook Viola's shoulder, bringing her from a deep sleep.

"Your angel again?" she asked.

He nodded. "It's those three Mexicans I saw with Lopez. They're coming back for him this morning. . . ."

He leaned forward and lightly kissed her forehead. "But we ain't gonna be here."

The travelers quickly gathered their belongings and the prisoner and left.

It was midday before they stopped to rest the horse and eat the lunch they had brought with them from Willcox. Slaughter unlocked the cuffs on Lopez's wrist so he could eat comfortably. He gave

Alvord and Lopez their share of the lunch before he joined Viola and Willie.

With his back to the two men, Slaughter began to eat, while Viola described some furniture she wanted to buy.

Suddenly, Slaughter jumped up and whirled around to glare at his prisoner.

Lopez's hand hovered mere inches from the gun sticking out of Alvord's holster. The deputy hadn't even noticed Lopez was going for the weapon!

Viola drew a deep breath to quiet her racing heart. If it hadn't been for the whispers of John's guardian angel, Lopez would have grabbed Alvord's pistol and shot the deputy and John.

As it was, it only took the cold, hard glare of John Slaughter to stand down the outlaw.

When they reached Tombstone, word came from Willcox that the three Mexicans had returned, demanding that their friend be released. They were well armed to make certain their demand was met. When they were told that Slaughter had outfoxed them by leaving town hours before sunup, the three rode away, defeated. Slaughter's clairvoyant power was once again proved correct.

With each incident, the legend of Slaughter and his guardian angel grew. Often, all it took was one glare from those hard, cold eyes and the simple words, "Git out of my town," to send a man running for his horse.

Usually, Slaughter's guardian angel gave him plenty of warning of whatever danger lay ahead. But such was not the case late one night when the sheriff was making the rounds of Tombstone.

Slaughter pushed through the batwing doors of the saloon. It wasn't until he actually saw the man standing just two feet away that he knew this man intended to kill him.

Perhaps it was the shock of that sudden revelation from his guardian angel, or perhaps it was the fact that the man was so close—but Slaughter didn't go for his Colt when his would-be killer drew a pistol.

Instead, Slaughter reached out, clamped his hand firmly atop the gun leveled at his chest, and slipped his thumb beneath the descending hammer. With his free hand, he snapped the cuffs on the man's wrist and led him off to jail.

"You son of a bitch!" the man screamed. "What they say is right. Ain't no man alive can kill you!"

John Slaughter served two terms as Tombstone's sheriff before he decided to put away his badge and devote his time to his San Bernardino ranch and raising cattle.

But the people of Cochise County wouldn't allow Slaughter to retire completely. In 1895, Slaughter was sworn in as a deputy sheriff by his successor, C. S. Fly. He held that position for the rest of his life.

Slaughter had always shied away from politics, but he was persuaded to run for the territorial legislature in 1906, and he won. However, when his two years in office ended, he did retire from public life. He returned to San Bernardino, where he expected to live quietly. Instead, he found himself again facing danger.

In the spring of 1914, the northern state of Sonora, Mexico, was torn by war between two governmental factions. Just across the border from Douglas, Arizona, and west of the sprawling San Bernardino, which lay both in the United States and in Mexico, was the town of Aqua Prieta. The town was in the direct path of the warring armies.

Daily, refugees fled over the border into Douglas to escape the warfare. In response to citizen fear, the U.S. Army marched into Douglas. Rumors now abounded that the United States intended to send troops into Mexico, too.

In the fall, the revolutionary leader Pancho Villa threatened to ride in and take Aqua Prieta—and Douglas as well, if the U.S. Army interfered in Mexican affairs in any manner. No one doubted this threat. Villa had ridden across the border with his troops on more than one occasion in the past.

It was on the Mexican portion of John Slaughter's ranch that Villa stationed his troops. Here he was within close striking distance of both Aqua Prieta and Douglas, where American troops waited. They had camped on the great mesas that provided high ground should an attack come.

John Slaughter, sitting on his front porch, could see both armies. To the south, he could see the Mexican rebels roping and slaughtering his cattle.

The years had weakened Slaughter's body but not his pride.

He ordered one of his cowhands to saddle up two horses. The man hastened to a nearby corral. When he returned, his boss was waiting, shotgun in hand.

"What are we intending to do?" the cowhand asked.

"Not we—just me," Slaughter answered. He knew he wouldn't need any help. He felt the presence of his guardian angel. "I'm goin' down south and jump Pancho Villa."

Slaughter spurred his horse to a slow lope toward the south range of his ranch. As he rode into Villa's camp, he felt the dark Mexican eyes on him.

At his guardian angel's reassurance, Slaughter

ignored the stares, rode straight up to the rebel leader, and said, "I want you and your men off my land. And I want payment for the cattle you've killed."

From their vantage point on the porch, Viola and the cowhand watched John argue with Pancho Villa, certain that this time he had gone beyond the protection of his guardian angel. However, when Slaughter turned back toward home, Villa and his men were packing their gear and leaving.

"Got twenty-dollar gold pieces in my saddlebags," Slaughter announced as he dismounted. "More than ample pay for the beef they ate."

Some called that meeting with Pancho Villa Slaughter's "nerviest deed." But Slaughter felt he was merely a rancher collecting the money due him, with a little help from a "friend."

When Slaughter celebrated his eightieth birthday, many speculated that Death himself might not be able to kill the old sheriff. But Slaughter knew better. In the late spring of 1921, he called a former deputy, Jess Fisher, and persuaded him to come to the San Bernardino as its foreman. Slaughter knew he was now too old to run his ranch as it should be.

Strangely, the last time Slaughter heard the call of his guardian angel, the warning seemed to touch everyone in the Slaughter household.

On May 5, Jess Fisher sensed "something in the air." Things seemed too quiet and calm around the ranch. Unaccountably apprehensive, he decided to spend the night on the San Bernardino rather than drive back to his home in nearby Douglas.

Viola admitted to feeling a bit nervous about ten that evening. A ranch hand hadn't shown up for dinner after he had milked the cows. She decided to go out and feed a flock of turkeys that the hand had also neglected, and asked Jess and another woman in the house to tend to the chicken coops that the hand had left opened.

While the three left the house, Slaughter remained in the living room in his rocking chair, reading a book. He regretted his lack of mobility in old age, but there was no bitterness. He had lived a long and good life.

Suddenly he felt that old familiar sense of danger; the whispering voice asked for the old .45 Colt he had used during his two terms as Tombstone's sheriff.

Slaughter pushed himself from the rocker, crossed the room, and lifted the old pistol from where it hung over the fireplace. He opened the cylinder and loaded the weapon.

Three shots exploded like thunder outside the house.

Slaughter rushed to the front door. On the ground lay Jess Fisher—dead.

Viola and the other woman had seen the shooting. The missing ranch hand and one of his friends, who also worked on the San Bernardino, had emerged from a bunkhouse. Three shots had been fired.

Later the two hands surrenderd to local authorities. Investigation revealed that the two had not killed the ranch foreman. However, they had aided a third man, Arcadio Chavez, and were tried and convicted of second-degree murder.

Chavez made his escape over the border. In Aqua Prieta, believing himself safe from the U.S. judicial system, he told Mexican law-enforcement authorities that he had killed Fisher and had intended to kill Slaughter, too, then rob the house.

"He came to the door and I had him in my rifle sights. My finger was on the trigger, but seeing him just standing there with his gun, I couldn't kill him. I stole some horses and ran," Chavez admitted.

John Slaughter's guardian angel had once more protected him. Chavez was tried by the Mexican courts and found guilty.

Fisher's murder took its toll on John Slaughter. He gave up ranch life and moved into Douglas with Viola.

On February 15, 1922, after a day's visit to San Bernardino, Slaughter returned to his Douglas home complaining of a headache. Viola called a doctor, who came to the house and remained with Slaughter until after midnight, when he finally drifted into a quiet rest.

At five o'clock that morning, Viola quietly entered the room and found that her husband had died peacefully in his sleep. Because of the strange and mysterious presence that had guarded and protected him, John Slaughter went down in history as the man no man could kill. . . .

Invitation to
a Demon

Matthew Hensley desperately wanted his sweetheart back. When all else failed, he turned to the black arts for help.

This tale of terror took place in an apartment complex in a major western city. All the names have been changed, with the exception of Captain Kevin Randle, who has been investigating reports of the supernatural and UFOs for over a decade.

Matthew was shocked and devastated when his girl friend, Randi Anderson, suddenly told him that their relationship was over. Matthew wasn't ready to lose Randi for any reason—and he was willing to try anything to win her back.

Matthew Hensley, a tall, well-built, handsome young man, had never lacked for female companionship. But this was the first time he had fallen in love. At twenty-four, he'd found the woman he wanted to marry.

Randi was lovely—tall and slender, with long

brown hair and large dark eyes. She was also the most intelligent, independent woman Matthew had ever known. She was right for him; and he was sure he was right for her, too.

With the pain of a lost love numbing his thoughts, Matthew wandered aimlessly around the city. He found himself in a bookstore, looking first at science-fiction books, then at mysteries, which he usually enjoyed. But today none of the books appealed to him . . . until he found himself in the occult section. There he spotted a bright red book whose jacket proclaimed it would make him rich, famous, and loved—whatever he desired. He had only to select the right spell and follow the ritual. Matthew picked up the book. On the cover was a picture of a naked woman kneeling in front of a pentagram; inside were photos of initiation ceremonies of witches, also naked, with their hands bound behind them. It seemed harmless enough— even silly. Matthew bought the book.

Back in his apartment in a major Colorado city, Matthew made dinner, then picked up the little red book and began to read while he ate.

The book wasn't very well written. Each section— one for riches, one for fame, and one for love— started with supposed testimonials from those who had successfully used the spells. He was amused by the "lovers" section, until he found the story about the man who had won back his girl friend by using one of the spells. Suddenly, Matthew began to read seriously. Ignoring his dinner, he picked up a pencil and began to mark things in the book. It still hadn't dawned on him that he really was going to try one of the rituals.

Matthew wasn't the type who would be expected

to turn to the occult for help. He had always rejected claims of flying saucers, ghosts, and the like. In college he had studied general science. He had always needed to see some kind of evidence, some proof, before he would admit that something was possible. But he was in greater pain than he'd ever experienced before. At midnight, Matthew put down the book and made a list of things he would need, including black conjuring candles and a crimson robe. He had decided not to go to work the next day.

A little after nine the next morning he went to an occult bookstore that had everything from books to dried bats' wings. Matthew consulted his list and purchased everything he required—a crimson robe, black candles, a goat-horn headdress, a vial of animal blood, and a goblet.

Matthew thought the day was perfect for casting a spell—rain, punctuated with thunder and bright flashes of lightning. Back in his apartment, Matthew went to the kitchen and began the preparations for the ritual. First, using a piece of chalk, he drew a pentagram on the tile floor. Around it he drew a circle. Then he lit the black candles, dripping wax on the floor so that they would stand upright. Finally, he poured the animal blood into the goblet and put it in the refrigerator.

In his bedroom, he stripped off his shirt and jeans and put on the robe. He tied the goat-horn headdress over his dark wavy hair. With the storm at its height, Matthew began the ritual that was to guarantee him Randi's love.

Back in the kitchen, he knelt on the floor, in the circle he had drawn. Picking up the book, he read aloud, *"Mugus Sigsigga ag Bara Ye. Innin Aggish Xashxur Gishnu Urma."*

He took the goblet out of the refrigerator, lifted it toward the flashing lightning he could see out the window, and repeated his chant. Then, despite the revulsion he felt, he drank from the goblet. He tried to convince himself that it wasn't really blood he was drinking.

When he finished, he picked up the equipment and put it away under the sink, hiding it all behind the garbage can. The candles went into a drawer. Then, still wearing the robe but not the horns, he sat down to wait for results.

By five o'clock, Matthew had finished most of a six-pack of beer and was feeling quite foolish.

The next day, Matthew went to work early, hoping that by keeping busy he would forget Randi for a while. At his office, an employment agency, he found a number of phone messages from the day before. He returned all the calls, occasionally wondering if he should spend so much time on the telephone; if the spell had worked Randi might be trying to call. Each time the phone rang, he hoped for the best—and each time he was disappointed. As the day wore on, the less likely it seemed that she would call.

Later in the afternoon, Matthew made a few final calls, finished some paperwork, and decided to call it a day. For over an hour, he had managed to forget Randi.

Just as he was leaving, the phone rang. His first reaction was to let it ring, but then he thought it might be important. It did not occur to him that it might be Randi.

"Hi," she said casually. "Can I ask you something before you hang up?"

"I wouldn't hang up," Matthew said. "I'd never hang up on you."

"Oh," Randi teased. "Then maybe I should ask you something else?"

A thousand things ran through his mind. He wasn't sure how to react. But he wanted Randi—more than anything else in the world.

Cautiously he said, "You can ask me anything."

"How about dinner? You could probably use a dinner."

"Dinner is fine," he said softly, trying not to let her know how elated he felt.

"I'll pick you up at your apartment," she said.

When he got home, Matthew decided he didn't want to go out for dinner; he wanted a quiet evening with Randi. Before she arrived, he put a roast in the oven. When the doorbell rang, he let Randi in. As he bent to give her a kiss, the doorbell rang again. Puzzled, he opened the door again, but there was no one there.

Matthew shut the door and they went into the large living room. He noticed that Randi had cut her hair; now it just brushed her shoulders. She was lovely. Matthew felt a surge of love for her.

He told her that he was preparing dinner. "I hope you like roast beef," he said, knowing that she did.

"Being with you is all I care about, Matthew."

He was thrilled. He was going to tell her that he loved her, but a sudden, angry pounding, like someone knocking, stopped him. It wasn't coming from the front door but from the wall near it. Probably some kids playing in the hallway, Matthew thought. He was about to get up to yell at the kids when the pounding stopped. Then it started again—this time, it seemed to be coming from his front closet. Matthew glanced at Randi, then started to get up, but the pounding stopped again.

He smiled, more out of confusion than humor, and said, "What the hell?"

"How long has that been going on?" Randi asked, puzzled.

"That's the first time I ever heard it. Must be someone new in the building."

She nodded. "What about dinner? I'm starved." She poked him playfully.

To a happy Matthew, it seemed that their comfortable relationship was returning.

The dinner went well. The food was good; the wine was excellent. They sat at the small dining table for a long time, gazing lovingly at each other over the two candles that had burned down to stubs. Finally Matthew put on some mood music and guided Randi to the living room. They sat on the couch, listening to the music, talking softly, holding hands. They both knew they would spend the night together. There was no pressure. They sat there, contented, enjoying each other, and finally went to bed about midnight.

The first poundings came at three. Matthew snapped awake, sat up, and stared at the darkened doorway. The pounding was rhythmic, coming at one-second intervals, and sounded like a giant bass drum. At first the sounds were low, but the volume built slowly until the windows rattled.

Randi reached over to take Matthew's hand. Her palm was wet, her hand trembling. Suddenly Matthew felt the hair on the back of his neck rise as a cold wind seemed to blow through the bedroom. Then the pounding died away.

"What was that?" Randi whispered. There was

something about the noise that had badly frightened her, something that had sounded unnatural.

Matthew searched the apartment. There was nothing out of place, except for a couple of magazines that had been tossed to the floor and a pillow that was on the glass-topped coffee table. He walked through all the rooms, turning on lights and turning them off. Back in the bedroom, Randi had turned on every light. She had also turned on the television, for the noise and comfort it could provide. For the familiarity of it.

"Nothing," Matthew said when he returned. "Nothing at all." He wondered about the magazines, but not very much. He sat on the edge of the bed, and Randi moved closer to him.

"But what was it?"

Matthew looked at her. "I haven't the faintest idea. I'll talk to the manager tomorrow, though. There's no excuse for letting something like this go on. Not at the rents he charges."

They sat up for another hour. Matthew convinced Randi that they could turn off the lights and the TV and go back to sleep. They were not disturbed again that night.

At breakfast the next morning, Randi was still quite upset by the pounding. Matthew assured her that he would speak to the manager about the noise and would call her. He then walked her to the elevator and told her he would see her that night.

Less than five minutes later, Randi was back. Her car would not start.

Matthew went downstairs with her and opened the hood. All the spark-plug wires had been pulled loose and all the hoses unfastened. Although he didn't say anything to Randi, he was greatly disturbed. The hood-latch release was inside her car, and she claimed that it had been locked all night.

Matthew offered to drive her to work. But when they got to his car, they found that one of the tires was flat. When he opened the trunk, he discovered that his spare tire also was flat.

Back at his apartment after driving Randi to work, things kept going wrong. It took Matthew nearly an hour to find his wallet, and then the money was missing. The pens and pencils he usually carried had been hidden behind the couch.

Nothing went wrong at work, but he spent most of the day wondering about what had happened. Several times he tried to call the manager of his apartment building, but the man could not be reached.

That night, he brought Randi back to his apartment. She was very tense and seemed ready to leave at a moment's notice. When Matthew questioned her, she said, "I don't like it here anymore." She refused to look at him. "I don't know what it is. I just feel like something bad is going to happen." Still she refused to look at him. "It's just a feeling in the pit of my stomach, like I'm going to be sick."

"Have you felt that way all day?" he asked, concerned.

Now she looked at him. "No. I felt fine until I walked in the door."

Matthew kept questioning her but she couldn't, or wouldn't, tell him what was wrong. He was afraid she was going to break up with him again, so he babbled away, hoping to forestall her. He suggested that they watch TV, but Randi couldn't relax. Finally, at about midnight, she said she was tired and asked him to take her home. Matthew noticed that her face was unnaturally pale.

Randi's two roommates were at home, watching a late movie. Both were in nightgowns. They scrambled from the room when they saw Matthew. He stayed only a few minutes, then went back to his apartment.

At three that morning, Matthew was awakened by three tremendous crashes that sounded as if someone had hit the side of the building with a wrecking ball. His heart pounding, he got up and searched the apartment. There was nothing out of place, nothing disturbed. It seemed as if he had imagined the noise.

But he knew it wasn't his imagination. He sat on the edge of his bed, staring at the floor, trying to figure out what was happening. Finally, he fell asleep.

The next morning, Matthew found another flat tire on his car. After he changed it, he discovered that the car wouldn't start. He opened the hood. The battery cables had been disconnected. He attached them and drove to work.

At his office, Matthew immediately called the apartment manager—who knew all about the poundings. The neighbors had already complained. Matthew added a strongly worded complaint of his own, and the manager agreed to check into the situation.

From that point on, the noises and disturbances were a daily ritual, occurring so often that it was hard to tell when one session ended and the next began. Nearly everyone in the building was complaining about the pounding. The manager spent days trying to locate the problem, but all he could tell was that the worst of it seemed to be coming from Matthew's apartment.

It was now two weeks since Matthew had performed the black-magic ceremony to win back Randi. She was still terribly frightened by the disturbances, still felt a sense of dread, but tonight she had agreed to have dinner with Matthew at his apartment.

Matthew drove to Randi's apartment and picked her up. As they headed back to his place, they detected a strange, foul odor in the car.

"What in the world is that?" Randi asked.

Matthew didn't know.

The odor became stronger, almost nauseating, then slowly faded. Just outside his apartment, however, they smelled it again. Matthew stopped there, with his key in the lock, suddenly afraid to open the door. He looked at Randi. She seemed frozen solid, as if she was too frightened to move.

Slowly, his hands trembling, Matthew turned the key and opened the door—and was almost knocked down by a blast of cold, foul-smelling air.

He switched on a light and entered the apartment, feeling absolute dread that he couldn't explain. He scanned the living room; nothing was out of place.

Randi stood in the hallway, afraid to enter the apartment.

"Come on, Randi," he coaxed. "Everything is fine. Besides, ghosts never hurt anyone, except in the movies."

He said it to be funny, but Randi didn't laugh. Slowly she turned to him, her face pale. "How do you know?" she whispered.

Matthew took her arm and tried to pull her inside. "They only have haunted *houses*. Have you ever heard of a haunted apartment?" he teased.

Just as he said that, a small ceramic cat, on the end table by the door, crashed to the carpeting and shattered.

Randi looked at the broken cat, took a step back, and said, "I want to go home now."

"But you just got here. Nothing's going to happen. Be reasonable," he pleaded. "I knocked it over by accident."

She hesitated, then relented and went into the living room. She sat rigidly on the couch, her purse in her hands. After a few minutes, however, she began to relax; she took off her jacket and set her purse on the floor near her feet.

After dinner, they sat down to watch a science-fiction movie on television. At about nine o'clock, during a particularly tense scene in the movie, the lights flickered twice, and went out. Thinking it was a general power failure, Matthew got up to look out the window. As he stood up, the lights came on again. When he sat down, they went out.

He looked outside; the streetlights were still on. He groped his way to the phone to call the manager. But the phone was dead.

Randi felt around for her purse. "Let's go back to my apartment."

"The lights will be back on in a minute. Besides, the elevator won't work without power."

"We can use the stairs." Then she cried, "Where's my purse?"

"Right by the couch," Matthew said. "Wait a minute and I'll get the flashlight." But it wouldn't work, even though he had recently put in fresh batteries. In a drawer he found the black conjuring candles that he had used for his ritual. He lit one and carried it into the living room.

As he entered, the lights flashed on and there was a gigantic crash that became a rhythmic pounding. Randi screamed, leaped to her feet, and cried, "Can't you feel it? Can't you feel it?"

Matthew didn't know what she was talking about; he didn't feel anything. But the pounding set up a similar hammering in his chest. He set down the candle and moved to the phone, but as he reached for it, it rose off the table and flew across the room. He stared at the empty table, the flickering candlelight adding to the eeriness, and said, "Jesus Christ."

Suddenly they heard a low moaning, as if someone was in great pain. It mushroomed into an earsplitting wail that shook the windows. All the time Randi was screaming, "I want to go now!"

The pounding continued, intensifying with every beat. Then the lights began to flash in rhythm with the pounding. Small objects flew around the room; magazines scattered across the floor; pillows bounced off the walls; an ashtray flew across the room and shattered a window.

Randi stood with her back pressed into a corner, her arms crossed over her face, as if trying to shield herself. She mumbled over and over, "Make it stop. Please make it stop."

Abruptly, the lights went out, the candle flickered, and all the noise ceased. By the dim light of the streetlamps, Matthew watched in horror as Randi grabbed her stomach and screamed as she doubled over.

Matthew ran to her. He saw that her blouse was bloody as he pried away her fingers. He unbuttoned the blouse and found seven cuts on her stomach. Three were horizontal and four were vertical.

Matthew cleaned Randi's wounds. Surprisingly, although there was a lot of blood, the cuts were superficial. In fact, they were barely visible. He took

Randi back to her apartment and, after trying to comfort her, left her quietly weeping in a chair.

Randi's roommates, Judy Sinclair and Susan Thompson, were greatly alarmed when they saw Randi's bloody blouse. They suspected that Matthew had assaulted her. Susan Thompson wanted to call the police.

"No!" Randi cried. Then she explained the bizarre events of the evening.

Neither Susan nor Judy knew what to make of it. All they could do was try to calm Randi down enough to get her to bed.

When Matthew returned to his apartment that night, he was horrified. Drawers had been emptied; doors and cupboards stood open; closets were in disarray. There was writing on the walls over the couch and near the television. The brown smears, which looked and smelled like feces, were vulgar and blasphemous. In one place it said, DEATH TO GOD.

At first, Matthew just stared at the walls. When the smell overpowered him, he opened the windows, turned on the vent fan over the stove, and sprayed the rooms with air freshener. Then, too agitated to sleep, he spent a few hours cleaning his ravaged apartment. Numbly, he considered the possibilities: burglars? vandals? homicidal maniacs? Manson-type cult? His mind reeled.

The next morning, Matthew went in to see his boss, Richard Edwards. They were close friends and often went to lunch together and played racquetball.

After hearing Matthew's detailed account of what had happened over the last few weeks, Edwards said, "If this were anyone else, I would think he was crazy. But I believe you."

"I thought you might have some ideas about what's going on," Matthew said.

Edwards straightened the papers on his desk. "I don't know what to tell you. I've never heard of anything like this, except in horror movies. You sure you haven't done something to alienate the kids in the neighborhood? Maybe they're doing it to get even."

Matthew shrugged. "There's no way they could have cut Randi."

"But you admit they could have rigged everything else?"

"I suppose. They'd have to be very clever to do it, but it's not impossible."

"Given that, and Randi's agitation last night, couldn't she have somehow injured herself without knowing it?"

"Well . . ."

"You have any other explanation?"

Matthew admitted that he didn't.

"All right, then. If something like this happens again, use a little objectivity. Look for the logical explanation."

Matthew left feeling better. His work went smoothly, he had a long, relaxing lunch, and Randi called to say that they both had been overreacting to a very strange but nonetheless explainable situation. Her roommates had convinced her that she was letting her imagination run away with her. Randi's attitude did much to reassure him.

Back at his apartment, Matthew spent the evening finishing the clean-up. The damage had looked a lot worse last night. The walls had come clean easily. The only things broken were the ceramic cat and one window.

That night, for the first time in weeks, he went to

bed relaxed. There had been no strange poundings, no broken dishes or ashtrays, no flashing lights. Matthew believed that whatever had been going on was over.

At three o'clock he was awakened by three loud bangs. Immediately after that, all the lights came on, as did the TV, the radios, and the stereo. The volume was so loud that it drowned out the pounding. Matthew leaped out of bed, turned off the TV in his room, and raced into the living room to shut off the stereo, radio, and TV there. Just as he finished, the alarm clock went off and the TV in his bedroom turned on again.

For several minutes Matthew ran from room to room, turning off the appliances, only to have them start again. In the middle of this, a banging came from the living room, near the front door. In his frenzy, Matthew ignored it. Finally, he began pulling out plugs and removing batteries.

Then the phone rang. It was the manager, demanding that Matthew shut off the noise; it was disturbing the other tenants. Further, he wanted to know why Matthew had refused to answer his knock.

"I would have answered the door, but I thought the knocking was more of the same. I didn't think anyone would be there," Matthew said.

The manager could hear the noise blaring in the background. "Turn it down," he ordered.

"But I can't," Matthew protested. "Every time I shut it off in one room, it comes on in another. I think it's the wiring."

"It's not the wiring," the manager shouted. "It's inconsiderate tenants like you. Shut it off. Unplug it. I don't care what you do, but shut it off."

"I can't." As Matthew said this, the noise died, as if to make a liar out of him.

Matthew went back to the living room, sat down, and watched as a lamp lifted from a table, hovered in the air for a moment, then fell to the floor. He just sat there, staring. Then, slowly, he realized he was staring at the book on witchcraft and spells that he had bought. He pulled it out of the bookcase and began flipping through it. Finally, he made the connection. The manifestations he was experiencing were somehow related to the book.

The next morning he began investigating. First he called the local newspaper, thinking that perhaps the man who wrote the astrology column might have some ideas. When that proved futile, Matthew leafed through the Yellow Pages until he came to the heading "Palm Readers and Advisers." He picked a name at random and called for an appointment. He was given an address and told to come at eleven that morning.

When he arrived, Mrs. Moira, the "adviser," told Matthew to sit and think about his problem. After a few minutes of silence, she asked him to explain it. Matthew was immediately impressed because the woman knew he had a problem.

After he had explained it all, Mrs. Moira said, "You have been visited by a poltergeist—a noisy ghost. They are famous for levitating objects, banging on walls, and making a general nuisance of themselves."

"How do I make it stop?" Matthew asked.

"The more attention you pay to it, the more noise it will make. If you ignore it, or just go away for a couple of days, things will return to normal."

Matthew asked a few more questions; then,

feeling better than he had in weeks, he left. He didn't know that almost everything he had been told was wrong. A poltergeist may be a ghost by some definitions, but according to the experts, it's really a noisy spirit, the difference being that a ghost was once a human. And poltergeists are more mischievous than evil.

Home for the evening, Matthew thought over the things Mrs. Moira had told him. Although she had portrayed herself as an expert in psychic phenomena, many of the things she had said made no sense when he analyzed them. She had claimed that the poltergeist couldn't harm anyone; yet Randi had seven cuts on her stomach, which suggested that the "ghost," or whatever it was, could hurt someone.

That night, things began again, about midnight. The kitchen radio, both TVs, and the stereo came on at full volume, and the lights began to flash. Moments later, the phone rang. It was the manager again, demanding that the noise cease.

Just as Matthew got the radio, stereo, and TVs turned off, a pounding began at the door. Apprehensively, he went to the door. He found two police officers.

One of them said, "Let's hold down the noise. Your neighbors deserve some consideration."

As he finished speaking, the stereo came back on at top volume. The officer looked at Matthew and said, "Turn it down."

"I didn't do anything," Matthew protested. "There's no one here but me."

The officers came in and shut off all the appliances. There was silence in the apartment.

"Keep it that way," warned one of the cops.

Just as he finished speaking, the kitchen radio

came back on and began to slip through the broadcast bands. Both officers looked at Matthew sharply. "How did you do that?" one asked.

"I didn't do anything. It does it by itself."

"Well, unplug the stuff and get an electrician in here tomorrow to look over the wiring."

Ten minutes later, with everything unplugged, the police left. As soon as they were gone, the kitchen radio began to play. Matthew ran out of the apartment and went to Randi's.

They discussed the problem, and Matthew told Randi about his visit to Mrs. Moira. Randi wasn't impressed. She suggested that Matthew consult with a priest or a minister. But Matthew refused; to him, seeing a minister was tantamount to going into psychiatric counseling, and he knew he wasn't crazy.

That decision changed within the hour. As Matthew drove home on Interstate 70, he encountered a large truck. As he moved to the middle lane to pass, the truck swerved. Matthew slowed, let the truck have the center lane, and then moved to pass again. This time it was as if the truck had hit a large puddle, except it wasn't water but a blue-green jellylike substance that splashed up on Matthew's windshield.

He turned on his windshield wipers, pulled to the side of the road, and stopped long enough for the windshield to clear. He considered trying to gather a sample of the material, but it evaporated too quickly. Then he started home again.

In less than a minute, he caught up to the truck. When he pulled out to pass, the blue-green gel splashed up again, blinding him immediately. He swerved, heard a horn behind him, and pulled to the shoulder. As the muck evaporated again, Matthew saw that there were no other cars on the road. Not one to honk at him, nor the truck that had splashed him.

He sat there for ten minutes, listening to the radio. When he felt that the truck had had enough time to get miles ahead of him, he pulled back onto the highway. Before he had gone two miles, the truck loomed in front of him. One moment the highway was empty; the next, the truck was there.

The sudden appearance so frightened Matthew that he pulled over immediately. About a mile ahead was a turn-off, and he crept down the shoulder toward it.

If he had still had any doubts about contacting a priest after the events on the highway, they evaporated when he entered his apartment. Every piece of glass and china that he owned was broken. All the furniture was jammed into a corner. Books, papers, cushions, clothes, records, and other small items were scattered throughout the apartment.

In the bedroom, everything was dumped over or torn up. On the walls were more scribbled words, just like those earlier, some of them backward so that they had to be read in a mirror. But the mirror had been broken.

Matthew was too stunned to think.

At seven the next morning, he picked up the phone to try to find some help. At first there was no dial tone; when he finally got one, there was noise on the line and he had trouble getting a call through; when someone did answer, it wasn't the number he had called.

Matthew raced out to his car and tore out of the parking lot. He wanted to get as far from his apartment as he could. An hour later, he found himself in the office of an Episcopal church, speaking with a priest.

After Matthew had told him of the recent events, Father Bob asked if he might come to Matthew's apartment later that afternoon. Matthew was enormously relieved. Then Father Bob added, "I'm not that familiar with this sort of phenomenon. But I have a friend who is—if you don't mind my bringing him along. He has been studying such things for many years. If he can't help, no one can . . ."

Matthew went home and began straightening out the mess. A few minutes before two, Father Bob arrived. With him was Kevin Randle.

Randle, formerly a captain in the air force, had spent years investigating reports of UFO sightings and other phenomena. He had also studied demonology and witchcraft. Since his background was in science, Randle was able to bring the scientific method to his research.

Captain Randle surveyed Matthew's living room. Then he looked into the bedroom but didn't go in. Next, he went into the kitchen. He scraped the tile floor with his toe, as if he could see the remains of the pentagram or the wax from the candles. Then he turned to Matthew and said, "There are some questions I have to ask. It's imperative that you answer them honestly."

Randle took out a notepad and sketched the floor plan of the apartment. He could still see evidence of the things that had happened the night before. He marked them down, quizzing Matthew when he wanted more information, and added that he wished Matthew hadn't done so much cleaning up. Randle then took out a tape-recorder, turned it on, and said, "First I must tell you that you are not being harassed by a ghost. The things that are happening to you suggest a spirit—one that has never had human form." Randle paused. "What did you do to invite the spirit in here?"

"I didn't do anything. It just began to happen."

"No," Randle said. "It doesn't just happen. Have you been using a Ouija board? A book on witchcraft? A Necronomicon? Performing rituals? Reading the satanic bible? There has to be something."

Embarrassed, Matthew admitted his use of witchcraft to obtain Randi's affection, then confirmed that the manifestations had begun shortly after he had performed the ritual.

Now Randle was sure that it was an inhuman spirit rather than a ghost. He explained:

"Although the first poundings came earlier, the real manifestations happened at three A.M. That is practically a signature of the demonic. The destruction is another clue. Demonic entities want to do things that cause fear and anger. Destroying something that a person worked hard to get is a good way to create the emotions that the demonic seeks. Too, the injuries to Randi are quite significant—both the form they took and the rapid healing. It all fits in; this is a case of demonic infestation.

"However, this seems to be a relatively powerless spirit. That is, it's not one of the more powerful demons. If it were a major demon, this would be a case of possession. You're fortunate it's not.

"Another problem is that demons are liars. They'll tell you they are Satan, but each demon has certain characteristics that make it recognizable. Part of my job is to figure out which demon it is.

"People don't realize what a chance they're taking when they begin to play with this sort of thing.

67

Most people think that a mass-produced Ouija board can't possibly be dangerous. They don't know that by using such a thing, mass-produced or not, they are inviting the demonic to enter their lives, and the demonic doesn't require much of an invitation.

"Even the most simple of tasks, or most simple of rituals, can cause trouble. Sometimes people hold séances thinking that it's all just a joke. They light a black candle and begin to chant, not realizing that a real manifestation, and possibly a possession, can occur. After all, a séance is an invitation by a medium for a spirit to invade his or her body. Once that happens, a demonic spirit is going to be reluctant to let go. Unfortunately, people just won't believe that these things can happen. They see TV shows or read books about it, then assume it's only entertainment.

"And, to make it worse, there are so many charlatans out there." Randle paused, looking at Matthew. "You talked to a woman who told you all kinds of things. She ignored the clues because she didn't believe in the demonic. Almost everything she told you was wrong."

"Is there anything we can do now?" Matthew asked.

"We can provoke the spirit and force it to reveal itself. The only way to do that is with religious objects."

"I don't think that's necessary," Father Bob interrupted. "I can just perform the ceremony."

"When we're done," Captain Randle told Matthew, "I want you to give me the props and the book you used in the ritual. That way you won't be tempted to use them again."

"Do you think that after all this I would use that book again?" Matthew protested.

"You'd be surprised how many do."

"You said that all the trouble came from using the book. Why would I want to use it again?"

"It's not that simple, Matthew. You have, after all, invited the demonic into your life. We can force it out, but once that path has been taken—once you have used it—the demonic can influence you to do it again. It's almost as if it extends an invitation to you, and you accept it, thereby reextending the invitation to it. Without your book and various materials, it will be that much more difficult for you to get involved again. Likewise, it will be harder for us to rid you of it."

At a nod from Captain Randle, Father Bob picked up a book he'd brought with him and began the exorcism. In the Episcopal Church, the process consists of blessing the house; rather than attempt to drive out the demonic spirit, it tries to fill the house with God. Because demons fear nothing but God, prayers and religious objects will drive them away.

When Father Bob finished his prayers, he blessed the people in the apartment and declared it free of all spirits. Captain Randle then turned to Matthew and said, "I would like to have that material now."

Matthew hesitated. "How is this going to change my relationship with Randi?"

"If it's a good relationship, one full of love and giving, it won't change very much," Captain Randle replied. "If, on the other hand, your reconciliation with her is just the result of the demonic, then the relationship will probably fall apart. With positive influence and love, you should be able to change that, but don't call on black magic to help. You've seen the trouble it can cause, and there's no guarantee that you'll get a lesser demon next time . . . In fact, it could even be worse."

"How?"

"The demonic can kill," Captain Randle said slowly. "There are a number of cases of possession that have ended in the death of the possessed. Of course, that is what the demon is trying to do. That, and cause fear."

"How?" Matthew asked again.

"By making the possessed person stop eating. Or begin drinking. Anything that's bad for the body. The stronger the demon, the quicker it can happen."

"You're just trying to scare me."

"I'm trying to impress on you the danger of the demonic. It is not something to be toyed with. The results can be disastrous. Fatal."

For the next few hours they discussed what had happened. Captain Randle told Matthew about some of the cases of possession he had encountered in his investigations, and stressed how important it was that Matthew stay away from the black arts, now that the demon was gone.

Just as Father Bob and Captain Randle were about to leave, the phone rang. Matthew answered it. At first he heard nothing but buzzes and static, as though the connection was about to fail. He strained to hear, then suddenly realized it was Randi calling. She was terrified. Through the static, Matthew finally understood what was happening. The demon had fled his apartment—and was now in Randi's!

Matthew, Father Bob, and Captain Randle raced across town to Randi's. As they pulled up in front of her apartment building, they heard the pounding over the din of her stereo and TV.

They rushed up to the second-floor apartment,

then stopped outside the door. From inside came a loud, rhythmic pounding. Over the noise, Matthew shouted, "What happened?"

"Your demon moved to a new location," Captain Randle said.

"But I thought they had to be invited."

"They do, but you invited it into your life. When we chased it out of your house, it moved here. Your invitation could be considered to extend to Randi."

Suddenly the pounding intensified. Matthew knocked on the door a couple of times, but with all the noise, Randi didn't hear him. Finally, Matthew got out his key and tried it. The door wasn't locked, but he couldn't open it. Both Matthew and Randle pushed, but still the door wouldn't budge.

Captain Randle took Father Bob's cross, placed it against the door and pushed. The door swung open.

They found Randi sitting in a corner beside her overturned couch, amid the rubble that once had been her furniture. She sat with her knees drawn up, her arms wrapped around them, her head down. She didn't look up when they entered.

Matthew ran to her. When he touched her, she jumped and looked up, then reached out and screamed, "Make it stop! *Oh, God, make it stop!*"

As Father Bob entered the room, things began to fly around. Glasses and bottles smashed into the walls. The noise of the radio and TV began to pulsate in rhythm with the pounding. Words and phrases began to appear on the walls, written by unseen hands.

Then the demon attacked Randi. She began to convulse and blood appeared on her blouse and shorts. It was obvious that she was in great pain.

Father Bob immediately began to read the prayers. At first the noise drowned out his words, then slowly the noise lessened and the pounding stopped. Randi fell to the floor, sobbing quietly.

When he finished in the living room, Father Bob moved to the bedroom, where the noise began again. He read the prayers quickly, never hesitating. Captain Randle followed, watching. As they moved through the apartment, the noise gradually subsided. Apparently, the demon was fleeing.

It took nearly an hour to work through the entire apartment. As the last of the noise faded and everything returned to normal, Matthew washed and dressed Randi's cuts. When the blood was cleaned away, it was evident that the wounds were superficial; although frightening and painful, they now were nearly healed.

Randi, calmed by the priest, was sitting in a chair, staring at the damage.

Matthew looked at her and knew how deeply he loved her. But his love was tinged with remorse for what he had put her through, and apprehension about their future. Now that the demon was gone, what would happen to them?

Captain Randle had said that any relationship based on love and trust would flourish. Matthew hoped so.

Rather than drive them apart, the ordeal brought Matthew and Randi closer together. With the demonic driven out of their lives, their love blossomed. Six months after the exorcism, in October 1972, they were married.

Matthew Hensley never dabbled in the black arts again. He didn't have to.

The Long-Distance
Canadian Ghost

~~~~~~

The following account, published here for the first time, was provided by Stephen Kaplan and his wife, Roxanne, founders and coordinators of the Parapsychology Institute of America. The material was taken directly from their tapes of the investigation. The names of the family members have been changed, but their terrified words remain as they were first spoken. . . .

Dr. Stephen Kaplan and his wife, Roxanne, boarded a flight to Montreal less than forty-eight hours after receiving a phone call from a very frightened Canadian woman. Rose Lemay had called the Parapsychology Institute of America to ask for help with an evil presence in her home. It manifested sometimes as a hooded figure, sometimes as balls of floating light. Doors opened and closed by unseen hands; ghostly laughter and voices were heard; strange odors wafted through the rooms; strange markings had appeared on mirrors. The situation had become so unbearable that she, her husband, John, and their four children had fled the house weeks ago and were now living with a relative.

John and Rose Lemay met the Kaplans at Dorval Airport and drove them to their home outside Montreal. The Kaplans had agreed to spend one night at the haunted house; the Lemays would stay there with them.

When they arrived, the Kaplans were not surprised to see that the house didn't look anything like the typical image of a "haunted house"; in fact, it looked warm, inviting, and well cared for, as did all the homes in the small suburban neighborhood.

While Rose made lunch, John gave the Kaplans a tour of the property. The first thing he pointed out was a short flight of cement steps that led up to a side door to the kitchen.

"That's where I saw a face looking in," he said, indicating the window above the steps. "It looked like a dead person. White hair and white skin."

"Where were you when you saw it?" Stephen asked.

"Sitting in the dining room. I saw it for only a split second. Then it disappeared."

"When did this occur?" Roxanne asked.

"Sometime in September. Around seven o'clock at night."

"How tall was the apparition?"

"I'm not sure, since I only saw the face. But if the thing was standing on the ground, it would have to have been more than six feet tall."

John added that his wife and his fourteen-year-old daughter, Molly, had often seen a "whitish person" walking around by the windows. Sometimes the thing would tap on the roof of the house. At first,

74

John hadn't believed them. "But one night at about one A.M. I was watching TV with my daughter, and suddenly it sounded like somebody took a ten-pound sledgehammer and banged on the roof. So I came outside and looked around, but no one was there, and there were no marks on the house."

John then took them to the other side of the yard and pointed out a large lilac bush that had new buds—very unusual for that time of year.

"This plant is about twenty-two years old," he said. "Every year, I saw this bush bloom in the spring, maybe May, and now suddenly it's blooming in October."

They walked around to a small cement patio behind the house. "This is where we had the gazebo in the summer," John said. "It's stored in the basement now. It's a screened gazebo with a plastic roof and a door that locks. Last month, my son looked outside and saw two birds flying around inside the gazebo. The doors were shut, and the birds were locked *inside*. My son had to let them out. How they got in there, I don't know."

When lunch was ready, they went inside. Over coffee and sandwiches in the small dining room, Rose and John told the Kaplans a bit about their family. Rose mentioned that her father had originally owned the house and had lived there until his death in September 1974.

Stephen assured the Lemays that he and Roxanne would do their best to discover the cause of the problem. He then explained the very unusual experiment he and Roxanne had arranged with the well-known psychic, George Anderson, who was appearing that evening on *The Joel Martin Show*, a radio broadcast live from Long Island, New York.

Anderson had been quite successful in giving psychic readings over the telephone to people hundreds of miles away. Dr. Kaplan would place a call from the Lemays' haunted house to *The Joel Martin Show*. He'd brought along an amplifying device that would allow them to hear the radio program while it was in progress. The conversation between Quebec and New York would be heard live on radio by listeners in the New York area. To protect the Lemays' privacy, their name and hometown would not be mentioned.

When lunch was finished, Stephen set his tape-recorder on the dining table, turned it on, and began to interview the Lemays in depth.

John began. "One day I was reading in the living room. You know how you can see reflections in the TV screen when it's off? I just happened to look at it and I saw a figure come across the room and go toward the front door. It happened so fast I couldn't see exactly what it was, but it looked grayish or black."

"It wasn't your wife or daughter walking by?" Stephen asked. "Or a reflection of something outside?"

John Lemay shook his head. "I turned to look, but there was nothing there. Another time, my wife and I were watching TV. No one was in the kitchen. But we heard a loud squeak, like someone had passed their finger over a pile of wet dishes. About ten minutes later, I heard a noise from the cupboard where I keep my barbecue utensils; it sounded like they were all rattling together."

"When did these events begin?" Stephen asked.

"Early August. The strange thing is that my family would hear all kinds of noises, but I wouldn't hear them until a week or two later."

Stephen was intrigued; he couldn't recall any other case where this had happened.

"At first," John said, "when I didn't hear anything, I thought they were crazy. But then I'd hear it too. But I know I'm not nuts."

Dr. Kaplan smiled. "If Roxanne and I thought you all were, we wouldn't be here."

"Well, you do begin to question your sanity after a while," Rose said. "It was maddening because we were hearing it and he wasn't."

"About three weeks ago," John continued, "my son and I were arguing because he wouldn't mow the lawn. He stomped out of the house, and Rose and I started arguing about him. Then suddenly we heard a growl. Rose said to me, 'Did you do that?' but I hadn't."

"I heard the thing speak, too," Rose said. "One morning while my daughter and I were doing dishes in the kitchen, I heard a voice say 'I want one.' I don't know what it meant." She paused. "It couldn't have been my daughter—it wasn't her voice—and none of my other children were in the house at the time."

"How clear was the voice?" Stephen asked.

"It sounded like it was far away, maybe fifteen or twenty feet."

"What tone of voice did it use? I mean, was it commanding, or was it friendly?"

Rose shuddered. "It didn't sound friendly. It had a very deep voice, and I was frightened by it."

"Were any of the windows open? Could you have heard someone outside?"

Rose shook her head. "They were all closed. That was the last straw for me. I knew I had to do something. I wasn't eating or sleeping. I'd lost eleven pounds by then—and my daughter had lost weight too. That's about the time we decided to get out of the house."

"We were under a great deal of tension," John added. "Sometimes the entire family would be up for twenty-four hours straight. We weren't eating right, either. No one had much of an appetite."

"It had been going on that way for two months," Rose said. "We were all very frightened . . . especially when we heard it breathing." She paused. "I tried to get it on tape once, but I couldn't."

"Where were you when you heard it?" Stephen asked.

"In my daughter Molly's bedroom."

At Stephen's request, Rose took him and Roxanne to Molly's room. It looked like a typical teenage girl's room, with pink curtains and bedspread, school banners over the dresser mirror, and a silver-spangled baton in the corner.

"I was in here with Molly, John, Jr., and little Gordon," Rose said. "We heard it coming down the hallway toward us, walking and breathing really heavy, like a person who has breathing problems."

"Like an asthmatic wheezing?" Roxanne asked.

"Yes. It was the first time I'd heard it make noise in a long time; I wanted to record it. I told Molly to go find our cassette recorder, but she and the younger children were too terrified to move."

"Could you tell how tall the apparition was by where the breathing was coming from?" Stephen asked.

"Well, it seemed to come from above, so it would have to have been taller than me. I'd say maybe five-foot-eight or even five-ten."

"Where did your father stay when he was alive?" Stephen asked suddenly.

"He slept in the bedroom next door." Rose led them to it. "This is the master bedroom; it's been John's and mine since Dad died."

The bedroom was furnished simply with a large double bed, a matching chest of drawers, and a mirrored vanity.

Stephen walked around the room, touching the furniture as though he hoped to pick up psychic impressions. "What did he die of?"

"A breathing problem," Rose said sadly. "The night he died, he just couldn't breathe." She sighed. "I had to rush him to the hospital."

"What was the exact cause of death?"

"The doctors said he died of a heart attack," John replied. "But he had struggled so much with his breathing that he'd busted a vein in his lung. That's what brought on the heart attack."

"So, in essence, the breathing problem is what killed him," Stephen said. "Rose, did this breathing sound that you and the children heard remind you of your father?"

"No."

"Can you describe your father for me?"

"He was about five-foot-seven, a hundred twenty pounds, grayish black hair . . ."

"And he was a veteran," John added. "He had lost his right leg during the war."

"Did he wear an artificial leg?" Stephen asked.

"He had one," John said, "but he very seldom wore it. He'd only put the leg on if he was going out."

"He used crutches around the house," Rose explained.

Stephen and Roxanne exchanged glances, remembering the banging sounds the Lemays had mentioned. Would crutches sound like banging on

79

the wooden floors? Could the apparition be Rose's father trying to get their attention, rather than some evil demon as the Lemays seemed to think?

John led everyone out of the bedroom and into the bathroom. "I want to tell you what happened in here," he said, picking up an ordinary-looking bathroom scale. "I bought this in May, and it worked perfectly. Then, suddenly, a month or two ago it started jamming at 260 pounds. Now, I'm the heaviest one in the house and I only weight 184. But at least three different times I found this scale jammed at 260—jammed so badly that I needed pliers to readjust it."

"When that started happening," Rose said, "I figured, well, that's what the ghost weighs. And that scared me."

"That doesn't necessarily mean that the apparition weighs 260," Stephen said. "It just means that some force turned the knob until it stuck at that number."

"I never thought of that," Rose said, seeming relieved.

When they returned to the dining room, Rose told Stephen that her daughter, Molly, had actually seen the apparition. "One afternoon we were sitting on the sofa watching television. My oldest son, Anthony, came in the front door and went into the hall, heading toward the bathroom. Molly looked down the hall from where she was sitting, to make sure Anthony wasn't going into her room—you know how teenagers are—and her face went white as a ghost. She said, 'Mommy, there's something in my room.' I looked, but I didn't see anything. But she insisted that she saw a black figure with a hood. My daughter is a very sensitive person, sometimes she knows what you're going to say before you say it. I guess you could say she's precognitive."

Stephen was beginning to think he should be talking to Molly. In documented cases of poltergeist phenomena, there is often a young teenager in the house. Some researchers believe that a child going through puberty unconsciously sends out tremendous amounts of uncontrolled energy, which could be responsible for some of the poltergeist activity.

"Would Molly agree to come here to the house to be interviewed?" Stephen asked. "Or is she too frightened to be here even for a day?"

"I don't know," Rose said. "She's staying at my sister-in-law's house. I'll call and ask her."

While Rose went to make the call, John told Stephen about another mysterious, disturbing manifestation. "We first saw it on Rose's birthday. She had had a feeling that something was going to happen that day. She was so scared that she asked me to stay home from work, which I did, and we kept the kids home from school. That morning, we found fingerprints on the hall mirror."

John led Stephen and Roxanne to a large, plain wall mirror hanging outside the bathroom. "There were three fingerprints down here at the bottom of the mirror. And Rose told me that the day before, she and Molly had seen eight fingerprints in the same spot and had cleaned them off. What was so unusual was that these weren't normal fingerprints. The first thing I did was have everyone in the house put their fingers next to the three prints on the mirror. Nobody's came even close to matching. These prints were—how can I describe it? We have flesh on our fingers. These were like the impression of skeleton fingers."

Roxanne asked John to pose with his fingers on the spot where the prints had appeared on the mirror. While she took a photograph, Stephen measured the distance from John's hand on the mirror to the floor.

"It's fifty-six inches—four-foot-eight." He looked at John. "Are you sure one of the kids couldn't have reached up and streaked the mirror?"

"No. They weren't human prints," John insisted. "Anyway, it kept happening after that. We found those prints on the mirror about every other day, always in the morning when we first got up. Every day Rose cleaned them off, but then they'd be back again."

"Is that the only thing that happened on your wife's birthday?"

"No, there was something else. My new watch suddenly went crazy. The second hand started moving backward! That really scared me. And then that night the dog started barking and howling like mad, but we didn't see anything."

At that point Rose returned and informed the Kaplans that Molly had agreed to come over and talk with them. While John went to pick her up, Rose told the Kaplans about another disturbing incident that had occurred on her birthday.

"The kids were turning the television channels and I spotted a Catholic mass on one channel. So I said to them, 'Leave that on, that's nice. We'll listen to that for a while.' So I was watching the mass—it was on a regular channel, not one of the cable channels—and suddenly the TV switched itself to cable. No one was near the set; it just changed by itself—and you have to press two buttons to get cable. By the time they got it back to the original channel the mass had ended."

"Rose, you mentioned on the phone that you had had a priest come over to bless the house. Did you tell him what was going on here?" Stephen asked.

"Yes. He didn't say whether he believed me, but he told me that I shouldn't try to fight it alone. He said I should give everything to God. Then he walked around the house and gave it a general blessing. My daughter and I had also gotten holy water from the church and sprinkled it around the house. But nothing helped. In fact, I got the impression that the ghost was annoyed."

Rose paused for a few moments, then said, "I just remembered something else . . . it's even more bizarre. It happened one day when I was very upset. A relative of mine had told me on the phone that she couldn't put us up at her house, and I felt that I had no place to go. I was sitting on the sofa, crying, while a soap opera played on the TV. Suddenly, I couldn't hear the sound of the show anymore. The picture was still there, but instead of the actors talking I heard a loud, strong heartbeat coming out of the set. My daughter turned to me and said, 'Mom, why are you afraid? It just means that somebody's thinking about you.'"

"Did you ask her what she meant by that?"

"Yes, but she couldn't explain."

"Maybe your daughter has more of an instinct about this thing than we realize. This might be a good presence in your house—one that is trying to contact you lovingly—but because of your fear of the unknown, you've misinterpreted the whole thing."

Rose disagreed. She was convinced that the mysterious presence in her home was an evil one.

When John came in with Molly, Rose served dinner. Afterward, Stephen and Roxanne interviewed Molly in the living room. A bright, attractive girl, she was in ninth grade, got good grades, and liked to teach baton twirling to the younger children after school.

"What was the first unusual thing you experienced in the house?" Stephen asked.

"It was a dragging sound, like someone who had something wrong with his foot."

Or someone who was missing a leg, Stephen thought. It was beginning to seem that the Lemays were being haunted by Rose's late father.

Molly then told Stephen that she had heard a knocking sound coming from outside her bedroom window; she had felt an unseen presence stroking her hair; she had felt her pillow vibrate when she tried to sleep; and she had felt something pull the end of the blanket when she and her mother were sleeping on the living-room floor one morning.

"Why were you sleeping on the floor?" Stephen asked.

"We were too scared to sleep in the back rooms after everything that had happened. My mother and I felt safer in the living room."

"Why do you think something would drag or tug at the blanket like that?" Stephen wanted to see what kind of insight Molly had into the motivation behind the occurrences.

"To wake us up, to get our attention," she replied.

"What else did you see or hear?"

"One morning, I was in the bathroom, washing my hair for school. As I was bending over, I saw something that was white, from the knees down, with gray feet."

"Were they male or female legs?"

"I don't know; it had a white gown."

"What did the feet do?"

"They were walking out of the bathroom."

"Did you follow it?"

"No; I stayed and finished washing my hair. I told my sister about it later."

It didn't sound as though Molly had been particularly disturbed by this strange apparition. Roxanne thought that perhaps Molly had become so familiar with the apparition that it no longer frightened her.

Stephen asked Molly to make a sketch of the apparition. As she drew it, she remembered that it had been barefoot and that the feet had looked medium-sized. After she finished the sketch, Stephen asked her to describe the black-hooded figure she had seen in her room one night.

"It looked about six feet tall," she said. "I couldn't see the face, though; it was covered by a black hood."

"Was it walking when you saw it?" Stephen asked.

"No. It looked like it was peeking out into the hall from the corner next to my bed."

Stephen asked Molly to go to her room and stand in the same position as the apparition had, while he and Roxanne sat on the couch and looked down the hall toward Molly's room to duplicate the view she had had that evening. Molly peered out at them, with just her head and her left shoulder visible. "It was like this," she said.

"When you saw this figure, did you turn to your mother and say, 'Look at that!'?"

"No. I didn't want to get my younger brothers nervous, so I told my mother about it later."

The Kaplans thought this was remarkably calm behavior for a young girl who had seen a mysterious black-hooded figure in her bedroom.

"Your mother told us that you were spat on," Stephen said. "Can you tell us about that?"

"I was lying on the floor watching TV and I had my shorts on. When I got up, the back of my shorts were all wet."

"Couldn't it have been perspiration?"

"No; it was all slimy."

"Did you hear a spitting sound?"

"No."

"Then what made you think it was spit, and not just water spilled on the floor or something?"

"Because of all the other things that had been happening in the house."

Rose and John then added that they had also found traces of a slimy substance around the house at various times. Desperate for help, they'd called a local psychic-research group. The group sent three mediums to the Lemay house—two men and a woman. After walking through the house, they claimed that the slimy substance could have been "spiritual ectoplasm," and came to the conclusion that the presence in the house was Rose's father. However, they did not have any specific suggestions for ridding the house of the ghost.

Rose had found the whole thing very puzzling. But she had been particularly bewildered when the woman medium, upon entering the house, had gone straight to the hall closet and announced, "There's a book in here that's very important." The woman had not said anything else or explained what she meant.

But there was a book in the closet—one that had belonged to Rose's father. Rose felt that if the book was so important, the hall closet was no place to keep it. She had asked John to take it to a relative's house to keep it away from the ghost, which she was still convinced was evil.

Rose then told the Kaplans about a ball of light that she had seen floating by the living-room door one night; and John told about a night when he was alone in the house and got so frightened by strange noises and doors opening and closing themselves that he fled to a neighbor's home.

It was now time to begin the next phase of the investigation. Stephen set up the telephone amplifier on the dining-room table, instructed John Lemay to sit in front of it, then placed his long-distance call to *The Joel Martin Show* in New York.

Through the amplifier, the Lemays and the Kaplans could hear the show in progress; Joel Martin and psychic George Anderson were describing the experiment they were about to begin. Finally, Joel Martin addressed Stephen.

"Hello, Dr. Kaplan. We're on the air now." His voice boomed through the amplifier. "Would you care to tell our listeners where you are?"

"Somewhere in Canada," Stephen replied. "I'd rather not say anything more about the location."

"Psychic-medium George Anderson has begun the process of automatic writing and is frantically writing now—that's probably the scratching sounds you hear. George can hear you; his earphones are on."

George Anderson then came on the line. "Hello, Dr. Kaplan. Remember—don't give me any specific information. Please verify now for our listeners that you've told me nothing except that we're dealing with a supernatural problem; you've given me no other details."

Stephen confirmed this.

"If any other person comes on the line," George continued, "in fact, before you put her on the line—" He broke off. "It is a female, isn't it?"

Stephen didn't know what to say. He'd expected that John Lemay would speak for the family.

"I feel more drawn to a woman," George explained. "The minute you came on the line, I got an impression of a woman having difficulty in the home: a woman crying, sobbing. Does that mean anything?"

Stephen was astonished. Anderson had described Rose's condition precisely. Dr. Kaplan motioned for John to switch places with Rose. John looked relieved.

STEPHEN: Okay, George. I have the woman. She'll just say hello to you.

ROSE: Hello?

GEORGE: Okay, don't say anything else. Whatever I say to you, *please*, emphatically, don't say anything except "yes" or "no." Just confirm me, right or wrong, with a "yes" or "no" answer. Okay?

ROSE: Yes.

GEORGE: Are you in your home now?

ROSE: Yes.

GEORGE: Have you heard . . . Have you been very emotionally upset?

ROSE: Yes.

GEORGE: Have there been . . . Have you been crying, or have you been hearing someone crying?

ROSE: I have been upset. I've been crying.

GEORGE: Did the . . . unusual phenomena take place in your home?

ROSE: [Pause.]

GEORGE: Is it . . . There's something missing from the house?

ROSE: No.

GEORGE: Are you sure?

ROSE: Yes.

GEORGE: What does a . . . Does a book mean something to you? A book, or writing?

ROSE: Yes.

GEORGE: Is it missing?

ROSE: It's not here.

JOEL: Then that would be considered missing.

GEORGE: I see a book being taken out of the house. A book, or some sort of writing.

ROSE: That's right.

GEORGE: Is the book hard-covered? Is it dark?

ROSE: Yes.

GEORGE: I see a dark, hard-covered book in front of me, being taken out of the house. Has someone personally written in it?

ROSE: No.

GEORGE: Are you sure no one signed a name, or . . . I see printing, but I also see personal handwriting.

ROSE: No.

GEORGE: Like someone marked off chapters, or . . .

ROSE: No.

GEORGE: It has to be looked into. I see a book missing out of the house. It seems to be . . . They say to me, "It's significant." This book.

ROSE: Yes, yes.

JOEL: The book is significant?

ROSE: Yes.

GEORGE: Something about going through the

book page by page. But something has been written in it, something has been marked out.

ROSE: Not that I know of.

GEORGE: Okay. It would have to be investigated, then, I would say.

John whispered to Stephen "What does George mean when he says, 'They say to me . . .' Who is they?" Stephen explained that George believes he is in communication with spirits on "the other side" who give him information pertinent to the person for whom he is giving the reading. In this case, George was giving Rose a message from somebody on the other side, probably a relative of hers who was trying to help her. Stephen added that the information George received by this method was almost always correct; George had a 90 to 95 percent accuracy rate.

GEORGE: Do you have any religious articles in your home?

ROSE: Yes.

GEORGE: You haven't taken them out, have you?

ROSE: No.

GEORGE: Good. Because someone is saying, "Keep the religious articles within the house." Are you the original owner of the house?

ROSE: Yes.

GEORGE: Has there been a passing in the house? Someone who lived there died; is that correct?

ROSE: Yes.

GEORGE: This person did not live there prior to yourself?

ROSE: It was the same time.

GEORGE: Did this person pass on unhappily?

ROSE: Yes.

GEORGE: Were you very close to this person?

ROSE: Yes.

GEORGE: I keep seeing things being either knocked over or disappearing in the house. Is that happening?

ROSE: Yes.

GEORGE: Do you feel threatened?

ROSE: Yes.

GEORGE: There's no reason to feel threatened. It seems . . . I'm picking up . . . Is this person related to you?

ROSE: Yes.

GEORGE: Was this person very ill?

ROSE: Yes.

GEORGE: Did their illness cause extreme, out-of-the-ordinary emotion within the home?

ROSE: Yes.

GEORGE: Does the name Helen mean anything to you?

ROSE: No.

GEORGE: Living or deceased?

ROSE: No.

GEORGE: Okay, I'll leave it with you, in any case. Did you take care of this person while they were ill?

ROSE: Yes.

GEORGE: I'm confused on this. I have to question you . . . Is it a woman that's passed on in the home?

ROSE: No.

GEORGE: Has a woman *close* to this man passed on?

ROSE: Yes.

GEORGE: The woman . . . I'm getting such a strong female vibration. The woman is the one who seems to be giving me the information. The person that passed on in your home is a male, correct?

ROSE: Yes.

GEORGE: But there is a woman close to him that has passed on?

ROSE: Yes.

GEORGE: Okay. That is who I feel I'm communicating with. I'm getting a strong female vibration and I had to place it either on the earth plane or in the spirit world. But there's a woman who gives me the information. She tells me about the book that's missing; that seems to be very significant. Would it be significant to him, or her, or yourself?

ROSE: No, to him.

GEORGE: Okay, she speaks about a book that's significant to him. She says keep religious articles in the home. Have you been waking up at strange hours of the night?

ROSE: Yes.

GEORGE: I get the impression that someone from the other side is trying to reach out to you in grief. Are you concerned about this person that's passed on? Are you worried about them being at peace?

ROSE: No.

GEORGE: Is there any hostility there?

ROSE: No.

GEORGE: I don't know. [Pause.] There's some sort of tension or hostility within the home.

ROSE: Yes.

GEORGE: Okay. Someone's trying to put peace, or . . . Why do I keep seeing a dining room? Is that significant?

Stephen and Roxanne exchanged glances. They were all sitting in the dining room right now.

ROSE: Yes, it's significant.

GEORGE: Was there any trouble within this dining room? Was there any out-of-the-ordinary activity in regard to what we're discussing?

ROSE: Yes.

GEORGE: The man who passed on had an important picture in the dining room. I don't know what kind of work is going on up there, but that's the place to work out of. It's the dining room. [Pause.] I don't understand it. Does a gun mean anything to you?

ROSE: Yes.

GEORGE: Is it still within the home?

ROSE: Yes.

GEORGE: Is it a handgun?

ROSE: Yes.

GEORGE: I see a small handgun in front of me. Does it have any significance to this man that passed on?

ROSE: Yes.

GEORGE: He didn't use it on himself, did he?

ROSE: No.

GEORGE: Just wanted to make sure. Does the name William mean anything to you?

ROSE: No.

GEORGE: Bill, William, Billy?

ROSE: Yes.

GEORGE: Is this person living or deceased?

ROSE: Living.

GEORGE: Would this person who passed on have known this man? Or would the woman who passed on? Someone from the other side calls out to William.

ROSE: Yes.

GEORGE: Were they very close?

ROSE: Fairly.

GEORGE: Are you frightened within your home for some reason?

ROSE: Yes.

GEORGE: Because of something you don't understand?

ROSE: Yes.

GEORGE: There's no reason to be. It seems that
. . . Has anything specifically severe occurred?

ROSE: No.

GEORGE: That's the thing. Someone says to me
that you're . . . I see someone, a long-distance run-
ner in front of me, and somebody says that you're
jumping yards in front of yourself. Would you classify
yourself as a little superstitious?

ROSE: Yes.

GEORGE: Well, it's explained in the form of
superstition. The person who has passed on—are
there any—undoubtedly there are—but are there any
photographs of this man on display in the house?

ROSE: Yes.

John and Roxanne looked at the dining-room
wall right behind them. There was a picture of Rose's
father hanging there.

GEORGE: I keep seeing a photograph of a man in
front of me. Is he an elderly man?

ROSE: Yes.

GEORGE: He is related to you?

ROSE: Yes.

GEORGE: Father or grandfather?

ROSE: Father.

GEORGE: Did he have any trouble with his heart?

ROSE: Yes.

GEORGE: Okay. This is your father we're speaking
about. Undoubtedly you're mourning him terribly?

ROSE: Yes.

GEORGE: There's a reason he's being held to the
house. I heard a voice calling, more or less, to let him
go, so to speak. Has anything been knocked over?
Knickknacks, articles of some sort?

ROSE: Articles have been moved.

GEORGE: Okay. That's the thing. I see motion of articles in the house. Knickknacks, or personal things, whatever.

ROSE: Yes.

GEORGE: I'm getting the impression these are all signs to let you know of their presence. But they tell me that you're being very superstitious.

At this point Joel Martin, the host of the radio program, asked Rose to put Stephen back on the line.

GEORGE: Dr. Kaplan, that book seems to play a significant role—I don't know why—but it means something specifically in regard to the situation going on. Whoever it is from the other side who's trying to contact her seems to feel that the book brings the answer.

STEPHEN: She was told by her father that the book should not leave the house.

GEORGE: The book is out of the house, though, is it not?

STEPHEN: Yes.

GEORGE: It should be back in the house. Definitely. Because that's the first thing I saw. The book should be back in her home, where it originally was.

George's concern for the book was eerily similar to that of the woman medium, who had gone straight to the closet where the book was stored.

STEPHEN: George, do you see any strange sounds or movements in the house?

GEORGE: Yes, I saw very strong movement in the house. In the dining room.

STEPHEN: That's interesting, because the Lemays saw a face in the window of the dining room. And we're sitting in the dining room right now. Also, a picture of the father is hung on one wall and a gun, handgun, is hanging on another wall within seven or eight feet of me. You also said the father had had an important picture in there, and he did. It's a picture of *The Last Supper*. It's right here, above my head.

JOEL: Speak about religious symbolism . . .

GEORGE: It seems that because of this recent passing in the family, someone's trying to reach out to her and they're more or less making their presence known. They might be a bit earthbound temporarily and then move on to the higher God-plane. So I would advise them most strongly to pray for the person, and pray that this person sees God's light and progresses spiritually. And for whatever reason the book should come back to the house. Okay?

STEPHEN: The husband's saying yes. [Stephen turned to Rose.] How accurate would you say George was?

JOHN: Ninety percent.

ROSE: Ninety to ninety-five percent.

JOEL: That's not bad for a few moments' long-distance phone call to Canada.

Joel Martin then thanked Stephen and the Lemays and began to close his show, and Stephen hung up the phone and dismantled the amplifier.

A lively discussion ensued over coffee and cake. Rose admitted that she might have been wrong about the apparition. After all, if it was her father (and some unidentified deceased female relative, perhaps her mother or her grandmother) trying to get in touch with her, it couldn't very well be evil. She didn't fully accept the idea yet, but George's uncanny knowledge of what was occurring in her home had made a great impression on her.

After questioning Rose further about the missing book, Stephen learned that it was an antique, titled *The Story of My Life: Marie, Queen of Roumania*. The dark green, hard-covered book had belonged to Rose's father, Anthony Tendler. Before his death, he had told Rose to take very good care of that book because it was very important. When Rose asked why, he would say only that the book *must never leave the house*. Rose was puzzled but honored her father's request. She had placed the book in a safe place in the hall closet. Neither she nor John had ever read it. It had remained in the closet until the mediums from Montreal had come to investigate.

The only other unusual thing that Rose and John had noticed about that book were two family-type crests embossed on the cover. The crests showed a lion and a unicorn. The Lemays had noticed that at least two of Mr. Tendler's other prized possessions had nearly identical crests. One was a glass beer stein commemorating the coronation of Queen Elizabeth II, and the other was a framed certificate of commendation for Mr. Tendler's service during the war. Since no one had read the book, no one knew what the crests meant. But John planned to go to his mother's house tomorrow and bring back the book.

George's comment about the dining room being "the place to work out of" was accurate. Mr. Tendler had spent so many hours at the dining-room table working on paint-by-number pictures. The large picture of *The Last Supper* was one of his works, along with the half-dozen other pictures on the dining-room wall. The handgun George had mentioned was an antique, mounted on a wooden plaque; it hung on the wall behind the living-room sofa. It, too, had been one of Mr. Tendler's prized possessions.

Stephen told the Lemays that what George had done in describing items in their home was called remote viewing. But George had gone beyond remote

viewing, because he had accurately described people
and events from the past and then recommended a
course for the future.

The Lemays were still not sure whom George
had been referring to when he'd mentioned William
and Helen. Rose felt that William might be an
acquaintance of her father's; the only Helen they
could think of was a distant relative.

Finally, the Kaplans and the Lemays retired for
the night. There were no unusual occurrences, and
Rose and John got their first good night's sleep in
weeks.

John Lemay called the Kaplans about a week
later. He and Rose had read the book and found that
it did have significance to them. The author, Marie,
was a member of the British royal family. She had
married the king of Romania, whom she had loved
deeply, but their families had opposed the marriage
and given them a hard time. Marie also suffered,
living in a strange land; she was discriminated against
because she did not speak the language well or follow
the local customs.

John described the story as being "the story of
our lives," meaning his and Rose's. Their families,
too, had opposed their marriage because of a difference in religion and background. Rose, who didn't
speak French, was still suffering from the prejudice
of some French-Canadians. Marie's story was one of
hope and triumph against adversity, and it gave Rose
and John inspiration. The book would certainly not
leave the house again.

The Lemays had moved back into their house
and were coping well. The phenomena had not

stopped completely, but they had slowed down, and the family was no longer so afraid, since they knew it was just Grandpa or maybe even Grandma saying hello.

One strange note to this case: When the Kaplans played back the tape of *The Joel Martin Show*, they heard a loud noise that sounded like a grandfather clock ticking over the sound of the conversation. When Stephen mentioned this to Joel Martin, Joel told him that several listeners had called the radio station that night to report the sound of a ticking clock coming over the air. But there was no ticking clock in the Lemays' home. And there was no ticking clock at the broadcast studio.

There is, however, a large grandfather clock in the Long Island apartment of psychic George Anderson. It's one of his prized possessions.

Under Directions from the Spirit World . . .

Texas's John Slaughter wasn't the only famous man who was protected and guided by a mysterious voice. Consider the case of Arthur Stilwell, whose "Brownies," as he called them, pushed and prodded and ordered him about. Under their guidance, he married the woman of their choice, became a financial wizard, and built railroads across America. But his greatest achievement was the creation of a city out of dust and swampland—a city that still bears his name: Port Arthur, Texas. A city built under directions from the spirit world.

Arthur Stilwell gazed proudly over the city he had built. Successful stores lined the streets and the main boulevard, which bore his name; beyond were picturesque homes and churches, and an impressive hotel at the end of Lake Sabine, with a two-thousand-foot pleasure pier stretching beyond it. Couples strolled arm-in-arm or rode in polished phaetons drawn by sleek horses.

There was industry here, too. To the south was

the harbor, with more than a mile of shipping docks. And, of course, there was the railroad. That had been Arthur's original dream: to build a railroad in the West—and he had succeeded. Rails now ran from Kansas City to the inland port he'd built, bringing people from as far away as Holland.

Stilwell smiled as he remembered all the people who had thought he was crazy when he announced that he was going to build a city in the Texas swamps. But over the years Stilwell had grown accustomed to people viewing his business ventures as crazy. No businessman wanted to invest in the projects of a man who believed in directions he received in his dreams, who risked millions of dollars on spur-of-the-moment hunches, who believed in supernatural creatures he called Brownies. But no one could argue with his phenomenal success.

It had not been an easy climb for Stilwell, despite the fact that he'd been born into an extremely wealthy family. His father, Charles H. Stilwell, owned the finest jewelry store in Rochester, New York; his grandfather, Hamblin Stilwell, was one of the builders of the Erie Canal and the New York Central Railroad and a founder of the Western Union Telegraph Company. Still, it was an unhappy childhood. Arthur was a sickly boy; he spent most of his days alone in his room in the family mansion, isolated from the world.

While other children ran and played in the sunlight, Arthur read, played solitary games, and lost himself in daydreams. But he wasn't really alone. . . . When he opened his mind to his daydreams, he saw things he could not explain—and he heard the voices of unseen playmates. An English nurse had once told him about invisible little creatures called

Brownies; when Arthur first heard the voices, he decided that was what they were.

When Arthur eventually gained enough strength to leave the house, his grandfather, Hamblin Stilwell, took him out into the world. Arthur even accompanied him on business trips to New York City. A frequent visitor to their suite at the famed Astor Hotel was Commodore Cornelius Vanderbilt, chief of the New York Central Railroad. Young Arthur loved to listen to the two men's long discussions on railroading.

One night the commodore asked Arthur, "What are you going to do when you grow up?"

Arthur replied without hesitation, "I'm going West and build a railroad."

His grandfather and Commodore Vanderbilt laughed at his precocity, although later Hamblin Stilwell would often repeat the claim to his friends. But for Arthur this was no fantasy—it was a decision wrought by the Brownies.

His mysterious sixth sense, as his parents called it, grew. When he reached his teens, they took note of it.

One day when he was about fifteen he came home from school and announced, "Today I saw the girl I'm going to marry!" He just *knew*. How or why he knew, he wasn't certain, nor did he care. All that was important was that he'd had a vision.

Arthur's parents were more amused than surprised. They were used to his daydreams and his uncannily accurate predictions of the future, so they accepted his statement as fact.

"I saw her in school today. Her name is Jennie A. Wood. She's small and has big brown eyes. I'm going to marry her in four years."

Arthur soon realized that he must find a way to support a young wife. Thus, at age fifteen, he ran away from home, with seventy dollars in his pocket, his childhood savings. In obedience to the voices he'd first heard as a child, he headed West, where he knew he would one day build a railroad.

Arthur Stilwell struggled through a variety of jobs until he received word that his father had lost his fortune in oil speculations in Pennsylvania. At his mother's request, Arthur returned home. The situation was worse than he'd expected. His parents had lost the mansion and were renting a modest house for thirty-five dollars a month in a poor section of town.

Arthur then learned that Jennie Wood had moved to Virginia with her family. Now, in addition to finding a way to support Jennie, he had to help his parents. He asked the voices for guidance, then fell into a dreamlike trance. The voices spoke . . .

Arthur went to the bank and withdrew his savings—four hundred dollars. With it he bought a print shop in Rochester, which he ran with one employee at night. During the day, he solicited work for his company. That netted him twenty-two dollars a week. Soon his success attracted the eye of a larger printing company, which hired him as a salesman for even more money.

That job well suited his talents, but advancement in Rochester was limited—and Jennie was still in Virginia. So Arthur went south in search of a new job and his future wife.

On the rail journey to Virginia, as he was reading the railroad timetables, a voice suddenly whispered to him. The few words made him realize that the timetables he was reading lacked the advertisements found in the timetables of the New York Central and other large railroads. It was a fantastic business opportunity, and Arthur reached for it the moment he arrived in Richmond.

Within a few hours he had a contract with the local railroad to print their timetables for free each month. He, in turn, would sell advertising and keep the money he made from it. Within a week he was providing the same service for all the railroads in Virginia; he had also acquired railroad passes from each line and received free room and board from the hotels that placed advertisements with him.

Producing the timetables and selling ads in them took only two weeks of each month, so he took a job as a traveling salesman with a Baltimore company. The two enterprises brought his salary to more than two thousand dollars a year—and his free passes on the Virginia railroads allowed him to travel to Petersburg frequently to court Jennie. Finally, with her father's approval, Arthur married her *at the age of nineteen*, thus fulfilling the prophesy he'd made to his parents four years earlier.

Over the next few years Arthur worked at several jobs and earned more money. Building a railroad was still his dream, but it would cost millions, and he had only twenty-five thousand dollars in his savings account. Then one day, while he was working for an insurance company, his unseen guides spoke again.

At the time farmers in Kansas and Nebraska were in great financial trouble. Because of low prices, corn was being burned for fuel rather than sold on the market, and mortgages were being foreclosed. The solution to those farmers' struggles appeared to Arthur in a vision of a map showing a dark flame burning a path across the United States. To Arthur, the answer was simple: a railroad built from the

Midwest to a southern port for export would provide a substantial reduction in the costs of shipping farm products to an eastern port.

And he would build that railroad.

To finance his railroad, he conceived a trust company that would sell homes for twenty percent down, to be paid in monthly installments over a ten-year period. Should the owner die during that period, the debt would be canceled and the house would belong to his heirs.

Over the doubts of his wife and the protests of his employers, who thought the venture was crazy, Arthur turned in his resignation to the insurance company. Within a month he'd packed his belongings and headed west to St. Louis to realize his vision of a southernbound rail line.

Arthur went first to see A. A. Mosher, a prominent St. Louis businessman. Mosher liked Arthur's plan and felt that basing the trust company in Kansas City showed good sense. He was so enthusiastic about it that he gave Arthur a list of Kansas City businessmen who might be willing to invest in the new venture.

Arthur knew that his choice of Kansas City was more than simply "good sense"; it was the perfect location for the headquarters of a midwestern railroad that would move south. But he saw no need to explain his ultimate goal to Mosher now, nor to any who decided to invest in the trust company. Once the company became successful and he had proved himself, he would purchase or build the rail line.

Armed with Mosher's list and his promise to serve on the board of directors of the new company, Arthur and Jennie went to Kansas City. Within weeks Arthur had obtained $180,000 from investors. Although it was an impressive amount, it was far from the million he needed to get the venture under way.

Arthur decided to go to Philadelphia to secure the rest of the needed capital. Although he knew fewer people there than he did in Kansas City, he felt sure he'd chosen the right city. He bought a Sunday newspaper and read all the lists of the boards of directors of the various trust companies in the city. He then made a list of all the men who served on more than one board.

Arthur then allowed his sixth sense to take command. He stared long and hard at the list—he even ran his fingers over the names. His fingers stopped over one name—William Waterall.

Pursuing his hunch, Arthur called on Waterall and made his presentation. At first, Waterall thought that Arthur had stolen the idea; at that very moment, the United Securities Company was using precisely the same plan. When Arthur assured him that he had never heard of United Securities and had conceived the plan himself, Waterall arranged for him to meet with the man who had conceived the same idea for United Securities.

The next day, Arthur, William Waterall, and the United Securities representative sat down together. Arthur explained how he had arrived at the idea, supporting each detail with files and columns of figures. It soon became evident that the similarity between the plans were simply coincidence. There was no question of theft.

Waterall, assured that Arthur's plan was sound, invested some of his own money and introduced Arthur to the Philadelphia businessmen who could provide the remainder of the needed funds.

Six months later, Arthur had the money and the

trust company was under way. And he had a friend for life in William Waterall.

Waterall believed in the power of Arthur's sixth sense. He once wrote to Arthur: "You were always a seer of visions; in other words, one of the young men who sees visions, something like John Bunyan and John the Baptist—visions that are far-reaching, after God and man."

Waterall understood how much Arthur relied on his hunches and dreams. Those hunches had led him to planning and financing his trust company. They had also led him to form a board of directors of an unusually large number of men. Many of the members were wary of this, fearing that the board would grow unwieldy. But in fact those members, many of whom were very powerful, often protected that infant company in its early days when competitors would have devoured it.

It was at one such board meeting in Kansas City that E. L. Martin, one of the directors, asked to talk to Arthur privately.

"Could I interest you in a railroad?" Martin asked as the board-room doors closed behind the last departing member.

Arthur's heart skipped a beat. He stared wide-eyed at his friend and business associate. Speechless, he could only nod.

Martin rushed on. "I own a franchise that will allow the construction of a belt line around the eastern and southern portions of our city. For three years I've tried to get backing and failed. If I don't start construction by this Friday—just digging the dirt—I'll lose the franchise. And if that happens, no one will ever be able to get it again."

"Friday!" Arthur cried. It was now Tuesday. Arthur realized that if he failed to move now, his railroad would be lost forever, because the big lines would make sure that the franchise was never picked up again. "How much is needed to get the line going?" he asked.

"Three hundred to three hundred fifty thousand dollars," Martin said hesitantly, as if he expected the matter to be dropped right there.

"Do you have a good contractor in the city?" Arthur had no intention of dropping the matter.

"H. C. Smith," Martin answered.

"Good. Get him up here this afternoon to meet with me," Arthur said.

"You've got the money to start the line?" Martin was amazed.

"No, but I've got an idea."

Hours later, when Martin returned with H. C. Smith, Arthur still had no more than an overwhelming feeling that this was the project he had been waiting for. His sixth sense had not revealed how he would realize his goal, but he didn't care—all he needed for the moment was that feeling. The rest would come to him. He *knew* that.

After studying a map of the proposed belt line, Arthur nodded and said, "All right. Smith, how many teams do you have?"

"Fourteen. All you have to do is give the go-ahead, and we'll start digging."

Arthur stared at the map. He was hoping for a vision, but nothing happened. Then he ran his fingers over the map, tracing the proposed route. He felt a tingling that grew stronger. "Smith, if I telegraph you Thursday night and tell you to put your teams to work right then, say about here"—his fingers

108

had stopped at a point near the existing Missouri Pacific tracks—"can you begin digging Friday morning?"

"If that's what you want."

Arthur rose and shook Smith's hand. "You'll be getting that telegram Thursday night, so be ready."

He then turned to Martin. "Hurry home and pack a suitcase. We're going to Philadelphia tonight to find the money to build that railroad."

As Arthur and Martin boarded the train heading east, Arthur's Brownies whispered to him. Suddenly he had a plan for selling the required stocks and bonds. That night on the train the two men and a stenographer worked like demons to draw up the necessary proposals and subscription forms.

Martin and the stenographer were exhausted by the time they reached Philadelphia, but Arthur felt fresh and well rested. His childhood vision gave him all the strength and energy he required. Finally, the simple statement he had made to Cornelius Vanderbilt was about to bear fruit—he had gone West and he was going to build a railroad.

After one day in Philadelphia, Arthur had obtained every cent he needed to build his railroad.

The belt line was built on one man's desperation and another's vision. Later, it was expanded to serve as a terminal railroad for the twelve lines that ran into Kansas City, and then a spur was built extending to Independence, Missouri.

But those six miles of track turned out to be far less profitable than Arthur had expected. The small stretch might have brought the collapse of the whole line, had Arthur not had another vision. This time, he saw people—couples and families—laughing as they strolled through a carnival.

Arthur wasted no time in building an amusement park halfway between the Kansas City and Independence terminals. Fairmont Park proved profitable in itself and for the railroad.

Arthur then turned to expanding his small railroad through Kansas City's West Bottoms to connect it to the only railroads still beyond the belt line. This time his obstacle wasn't unwilling investors, but the land itself.

Two formidable bluffs separated the West and East Bottoms, which extended all the way out to the Missouri River. Below was a narrow strip of land that connected them. The problem was that the strip was occupied by the Missouri Pacific's double track. And that line had no intention of giving up such prime real estate.

Arthur turned the problem over to his engineer. The man was skeptical. There was about a hundred-foot elevation difference to be overcome in a very short distance. At Arthur's insistence, the engineer took out his teams and surveyed. And resurveyed. And resurveyed. When the engineer concluded that it would be impossible to lay the desired rail, Arthur called in other experts. But they, too, felt it was impossible.

Arthur was about to give up. But then came the dream, and with it the solution to the problem that had dumbfounded the experts.

He awoke trembling with anticipation. It seemed too simple! Instead of using a direct route from his present terminal, he would lay rails through town, then swing toward the West Bottoms and make the connection.

After making some preliminary surveys, Arthur's engineer agreed that the indirect route would work.

Once again, Arthur's dreams had provided an answer to his problems.

But there was another barrier. Arthur would have to build a bridge that would span the tracks of three other railroads. As construction of the bridge began, Arthur was enjoined by the Missouri Pacific, which claimed ownership of the land on which the bridge was being built.

Without that bridge, the expansion was impossible.

Once again, it was one of his hunches that saved him. The day after he'd had the dream, Arthur had sought out a man whose family had extensive land holdings in the city. When Arthur asked if the family owned any land in the West Bottoms, the man had expressed doubt, but he had agreed in writing to sell Arthur any lands he might hold there for fifteen thousand dollars an acre.

Until the court action by the Missouri Pacific, Arthur had not needed to press that claim. Now, a search of titles revealed that the Missouri Pacific had overlooked a small wedge of land between their properties when they had acquired rights-of-way in the West Bottoms. That small parcel of land belonged to the family who had promised to sell to Arthur. . . .

Thus, at the age of thirty, Arthur had a total of sixty miles of track. He believed he had realized his original dream and fulfilled the direction of the voices. But the voices urged him on. Now there was another dream—to contruct a rail line to a southern port and provide cheaper export transportation for the financially pressed farmers of the Midwest.

The push southward began when Arthur's friend E. L. Martin suggested that their railroad, the Kansas City Southern, expand about eighty miles to Hume,

Missouri, and the coal fields there. Seeing a way to begin his still-unrevealed push to the coast, Arthur suggested that the line go even further, to Louisiana.

Then came the panic of 1893. Money was tight and people did not want to invest in a railroad. But, of course, Arthur had another hunch.

After some incredible financial manipulations involving promissory notes in America against an even larger promised loan from Holland, the money was raised. Arthur's railroad expanded to Louisiana.

It was there that he intended to stop. However, he soon learned that the Houston, East and West Texas Railroad was for sale. He rushed to New York and obtained an option on the line. If he could purchase it, he could extend his railroad all the way to the Gulf Coast.

He then sent out feelers to Philadelphia and Holland for financial backing as he primed his board of directors, preparing them for the purchase. The proposal was favorably received and its passage assured.

The night before the board meeting at which he was to receive the go-ahead for his plan, Arthur had another dream.

First, the voices told him to abandon his plans to purchase the Houston, East and West Texas line. They told him to search for an end to his railroad in the northeastern portion of the Texas coast. Puzzled, Arthur felt himself floating through the air, seeing the United States spread out below him. He saw not just the deep-water port he sought but an entire city located on the north bank of Lake Sabine. Bewildered, he stared at the awesome vision. The city was landlocked, miles from the Gulf of Mexico. How could this be the port terminal he sought? Then he saw a seven-mile canal from his dream city to the city of Galveston. But Galveston was already the major port for that area. Arthur couldn't understand why the voices instructed him to build a rail terminal when one was not needed.

Arthur awoke suddenly, his pulse pounding, his body covered with sweat. He was to build that city!

Just hours before the board of directors met, Arthur drew up a plan to dissuade them from purchasing the Houston, East and West Texas line and instead to invest in his dream city. The board members, knowing the strength of Arthur's visions, agreed to support him.

Three days later, with his wife and his chief engineer at his side, Arthur set out in his private railroad car for Sabine Pass and Lake Sabine. Though he had never been to that region, the layout of the land and the lake was exactly as he had seen in his vision.

"The first thing is to build a canal," he said as he looked over the swampland. When his engineer answered that he knew nothing about canals, Arthur told him to use the Suez Canal as a model. He then ordered a representative of the Kansas City Southern to begin buying land on the north bank of Lake Sabine—the exact location for the city revealed in his dream. That alligators and water moccasins now dwelled on that land didn't matter . . .

Arthur again turned to the supernatural for help when he hired a soil taster—a man who claimed he could taste the soil and tell what crops it was suitable for. The man's advice: rice.

Thus, Arthur formed the Port Arthur Rice Farm and started digging irrigation ditches to bring water from the Neches River about seven miles away. However, he still needed people to work the land.

He found the needed farmers by once more reaching across the Atlantic Ocean to Holland and offering immigrants property at forty dollars an acre. Not only was most of the acreage sold, but the soil taster's advice was proved correct: the land was extremely fertile for raising rice. The farmers' first crop was so lucrative that it paid for most of their initial investment. To handle the grain, two rice mills were erected in Port Arthur. Of course, there was the railroad to transport the crop once the line connected Port Arthur with Shreveport.

Everything about Port Arthur and the surrounding area seemed to Arthur to be falling into place too easily. He became wary. And he was not surprised when disaster struck.

The landowners of Sabine Pass wanted a thousand dollars per acre for the land needed to complete the canal to Port Arthur—land that Arthur estimated was worth fifty cents per acre. Without that land, the railroad and Port Arthur would be a complete failure.

After a series of court battles that eventually led Arthur to Washington to appear before the House Ways and Means Committee, he won the fight and the last four feet of canal were dug. Port Arthur was connected to the Gulf of Mexico!

On the day the canal was completed, the purpose of Arthur's vision was revealed.

A devastating hurricane struck the gulf. Galveston was flooded, its port useless. That same howling storm drove seven ships through the canal into Port Arthur, where they found refuge from nature's fury. From then on, shipping shifted from Galveston to the safety of Port Arthur and its easily available rail lines. Port Arthur continued to expand and grow.

Port Arthur, Texas—the only city ever located and built under directions from the spirit world . . .

The Corpse That Wouldn't Tell

~~~~~~

This bizarre murder mystery comes from the files of the Parapsychology Institute of America, founded and co-directed by Dr. Stephen Kaplan and his wife, Roxanne. The account was assembled from actual tape-recordings of the researchers' investigation. Although the participants' names have been changed (with the exception of the Kaplans) to protect the privacy of the family and their friends, this murder is a real case. All the details are true, including the strange, inexplicable ending. . . .

In early October 1976, Dr. Stephen Kaplan received a phone call from Meg Bascomb. She had heard that the Parapsychology Institute sometimes used psychics to locate missing persons and hoped that Stephen might help her. However, it was not a missing person but a missing corpse that she wanted to find.

The tale that Meg Bascomb then revealed was both tragic and puzzling. It had begun more than a month earlier, in late August. Meg Bascomb's best friend, Teresa Ferucci, had disappeared from her home on the south shore of Nassau County, Long Island, and signs of extreme violence had been found at the house. Teresa's husband, Vincent, had been arrested early the next day and charged with attempted murder. Vincent admitted that he had argued with his wife and then had struck her on the head with a heavy object. He also admitted to having placed his wife in the trunk of his car and driven out to Suffolk County. But at that point his story became vague. Vincent claimed that he had left Teresa, groggy but alive, propped against a fence in a vacant lot near the highway.

The police had searched for Teresa but had not found her. Meg Bascomb and the Ferucci children, Tina, age twenty-two, and Terence, age sixteen—were sure that Teresa was dead but couldn't imagine what Vince had done with the body. All they really wanted now was to find Teresa and give her a proper burial.

Touched by Mrs. Bascomb's obvious sorrow, Stephen agreed to gather a team of researchers and psychics to investigate the case. There would be no charge for the work. As a public-service organization, the Parapsychology Institute donates its services in exchange for the knowledge gained from the field research.

Three hours later, Stephen had organized his team and arranged for them to assemble at the Ferucci house in one week. The researchers included Roxanne Salch, the corresponding secretary for the PIA, who had researched many cases of strange phenomena; Fred Ford, a PIA member who knew a great deal about electronics and had studied parapsychology and ESP for many years; Connie Rockford, the recording secretary for the PIA; and Jo Tamerlane, head of the PIA's experiments in ESP testing, who had recently begun developing her own psychic abilities. These four members would accompany Stephen to the Ferucci home. Four more PIA members would meet them there: Pete Goldberg, an expert on archaeology and theoparapsychology (parapsychology as it relates to the Bible); Jack Krantz, a professional photographer and film historian; Faith Calvin, an astrologer; and Sandra Collins, an extremely talented psychic.

When Stephen and his researchers arrived at the Ferucci home, Meg Bascomb was there to greet them. With her were Teresa Ferucci's daughter, Tina, and Earl Logan, a close friend of the family.

After introductions were made and the group settled in the living room, Meg gave Stephen a small pile of letters that Vince Ferucci had written to his children. Meg had already shown the letters to a graphologist, but she knew that Stephen had studied handwriting analysis and she wanted his opinion.

Stephen looked at the first letter. "This person is an introvert," he said. "He's well organized, normally a positive person, level-headed, artistic, very dramatic and logical."

He altered his analysis when he saw the next letter. "This sample is totally different. The writing is going downhill; the thoughts are disturbed and disjointed. He's not clear in his thinking, and his ideas are not flowing well. However, he's still meticulous and accurate, rational, intelligent, and logical. The handwriting varies; it seems to change personality. It almost looks like a different person wrote this second sample."

Stephen then looked at the third letter. "It starts

out quite normally," he observed, "but this one paragraph becomes disjointed. He's still an introvert, but that paragraph shows a sharp, contrasting change to what I would call his 'other' personality. Then his handwriting becomes normal again at the end."

Meg then revealed the conclusions drawn by the graphologist she'd consulted. Vince's handwriting had indicated that he had two personalities: personality A, a highly intelligent, conservative, nonviolent man; and personality B, an individual who was below adolescent level, with the mentality and temperament of an enraged child. Neither personality A nor personality B would commit premeditated murder. The graphologist believed that the crime had happened at the spur of the moment. Personality B had suddenly emerged and committed the crime; afterward, personality A took over and said, "What have I done?"

"Vince once beat up Tina when she was a young girl," Meg said. "He knows he has violent tendencies, and he can usually control them, but I guess this time he wasn't able to. I think he knows right from wrong; he's not insane. He knows what he's done, and he knows what he did with his wife." Meg paused. "The graphologist also said that Vince is cagey and shrewd. That's true. He's also a great thinker." She paused. "All I know is that we can't find Teresa."

"We'd like to start by having Jo walk around the house to see what impressions she can come up with psychically," Stephen said. "Fred will go with her and record her impressions on our tape-recorder. When our other psychic, Sandra, arrives, we'll repeat the procedure."

Jo and Fred went to the master bedroom first. Jo opened the closet and looked at Teresa's clothes, still hanging neatly in place. The room seemed to be waiting for Teresa to return, but Jo was sure that Teresa Ferucci was no longer alive. She felt that the fight between Teresa and Vince had started in their bedroom, but that was the only impression she got at that time.

Jo and Fred moved on to the bathroom and then down to the basement, and Jo again experienced the feeling that Teresa Ferucci had died.

Jo and Fred then went back upstairs. As they were walking through the narrow hall toward the kitchen, Jo suddenly stopped. "I feel like I don't want to go in there," she said. "Give me a moment or two. I felt a cold shiver run through me." When Jo had composed herself, they entered the kitchen. "The feeling is gone now," she said, "but I definitely felt negative vibes in the hall."

They went through all the other rooms in the house, but Jo did not get any more impressions.

"I think the fight started in the bedroom," she concluded, "and Teresa was walking out the front door when Vince decided he didn't want her to leave. But I don't think she was killed there."

Meg Bascomb had not yet revealed the details of what had happened the night Teresa disappeared, because Stephen had not wanted his psychic investigators to be influenced by what she might say. Now, at Stephen's request, Meg began:

"Teresa was supposed to come to my house that night, but she never showed up. So I drove over here and knocked on the front door. At first, no one answered, but the door was ajar and I saw Vince turning off the porch light and rushing in toward the hall. I banged harder on the door and their dog began to bark. Finally, Vince yelled out, 'Who is it?' in a very calm voice. I answered, 'It's Meg. Where's Teresa?' Vince said that she was on her way over to my house and that he couldn't come to the door because he wasn't dressed. Of course, I realize now that he probably couldn't let me see him because the front of his shirt would have been covered with blood."

"As I understand it," Stephen said, "Teresa and Vince had had an argument and Vince had hit her over the head with something heavy. When you came to the door, he quickly switched off the light in the porch area so you wouldn't see Teresa lying there, and lied to you about Teresa being on her way to your house. He then placed her in the trunk of his car and drove out to Suffolk County where he stopped to purchase gasoline."

"He used a credit card to pay for the gas," Tina commented. "But he had at least thirty dollars in cash."

"That's very puzzling," Stephen said. "Why would a man who had just committed a violent crime use a credit card? He must have known that the credit slip would be proof of where he had been that night."

Stephen then questioned Tina further. She had visited her father in prison several times in the last month and had tried to get the truth from him. But he had told her a different story each time. Once, he had said, "You're not going to find her." Sometimes he said that Teresa was alive and would be found; at other times he said he was convinced that she was dead, simply because of the amount of time that had passed. Vince did admit to having beaten Teresa, but he claimed that she was alive when he had left her propped against a fence in Suffolk County.

Stephen thought about the possibility that Vince

had dumped Teresa's body into the ocean. "Tina, does your father know the water, the tides?"

"Sure, he's a fisherman."

"Does he have any favorite spots?"

"At least half a dozen—Shinnecock, Wildwood, Woodmere, Lindenhurst, Baldwin, Long Beach, and Point Lookout. I know the one in Woodmere the best. There's a pier there, and there are fishermen around all the time, even at night. But my father said 'no water' and that he didn't bury her either. He sticks to that."

"What kind of condition does he say your mother was in when he left her by the fence?"

"He says she was shaky, but that she walked to the fence from the car trunk, still talking to him. But he contradicts himself constantly. Another time he said that she was very, very shaky and he used something like a tarpaulin or a jacket to pull her out of the trunk. When I said to him that it would have been hard for him to carry her, weighing one hundred thirty pounds for one hundred feet, he said, 'I didn't carry her ten feet.'"

"One other thing," Tina said. "He knows the Southern State Parkway very well and all the streets between here and there."

Stephen took out a map and studied it, noting that the parkway crossed the length of the island all the way out to Montauk Point, passing Shinnecock along the way.

Fred then took over the questioning.

"What time did your father leave the house that night?"

"Between quarter to nine and nine-thirty. My brother, Terry, got home at nine-thirty. Meg left here at a quarter to nine. My father arrived at the gas station at ten P.M. The attendant testified to that yesterday in court. I believe the gas station was on the south side of the highway, so he was probably going east. He bought seven dollars worth of gas. His signature on the charge slip looks very different from his normal handwriting."

"And what time did he arrive back at the house?"

"Well, I discovered all the blood and my mother's partial denture plate near the porch when I got home, and shortly afterward I called the police. When the officers arrived, I started watching the window. At around midnight I saw his car go by. I told the officers, but they thought I was mistaken, they didn't think he would dare come back here after what he had done. But I know my father's car very well. He was headed east that first time I saw him. The second time I saw him was at about three-ten, when he went by coming *from* the east. He turned and saw me through the window, and I ran outside, with the police after me. My father accelerated, but then he suddenly turned into the driveway. I guess he realized that he had nowhere else to go."

"What time was it when you got home and discovered the blood?" Fred asked.

"About quarter to ten. I had left the house at six-thirty that night. My mother was home when I left, and so was my father. She was supposed to be leaving at seven-thirty to go to Meg's house to sign divorce papers, but Terry and I didn't know that at the time."

"So that's what got Vince in such a rage," Stephen remarked.

"No," Tina protested. "First of all, I don't think my mother would have told him that she was on her way to sign divorce papers, but even if she had, I can't see him getting upset enough to kill her. There were

123

plenty of times in the past when she had told him she was going to get a divorce, and he totally ignored it."

Stephen thought that perhaps this time Vince Ferucci had taken his wife seriously.

Meg and Tina then gave Stephen some additional information. Vince had told his children that he had indeed gotten onto the Southern State Parkway and had heard Teresa knocking inside the trunk. However, the police had not found any fingerprints on the inside of the trunk. Ferucci had also said that he had thought of taking his wife to a hospital, but he had never followed through on that; instead, he had allegedly left her by a fence near the highway. According to Tina and Meg, Vince was not worried about serving time in prison, because his favorite pastimes were sitting and thinking and watching TV. He could do all this in prison as well as at home. He felt no remorse for the crime, and claimed it wasn't his fault, although he admitted to having hit her on the head. He said he had wanted to go for her throat, but hadn't done so because Teresa was a singer.

Tina believed that her mother had been hit on the head with a frying pan. She had found one in the dishwasher, with something burnt stuck to it, while everything else in the dishwasher was clean. She felt that her father had hit her mother from behind with the frying pan as she was on her way out the porch door, because her keys had been found under a dining-room chair, where they likely would have landed if they had flown out of Teresa's hand.

"My father claims that he saw my mother outside in the driveway kissing another man, and that drove him crazy. He says that she then came back onto the porch, and that's when he hit her. But there's no way she would have come back in that door once she had gotten out to the car. My mother was afraid of him."

"Could Vince have actually seen a man outside with your mother?" Stephen asked hesitantly. "Did she have any male friends?"

"None," Tina said firmly. "She had gone to Paris in July. He claimed she had gone there to fool around. If you knew my mother, you'd know that's ridiculous. Everybody could tell you that."

Fred then asked Tina to see the area where all the blood had been found. Tina led the group into the dining room. The door to the porch was on the far side of the room. Tina explained that her mother's denture plate had been found by that door, while the keys had been found under a chair approximately four feet from the door. Next to the keys had been a clump of skin; Tina had thought it looked like it came from the inside of the mouth. The police had identified the skin and blood as being Teresa's, but they hadn't told Tina what part of the body the skin was from. The first thing Tina had seen when she looked on the porch was a rolled-up scatter rug completely covered with blood. She had then noticed dots and speckles of blood on the door, on the walls, and on a pile of old newspapers nearby. Although the room had been cleaned over a month ago, dark stains were still visible on the porch door. Everyone felt uncomfortable. None of them had ever been this close to a murder scene before.

When Tina had discovered the blood, she had let out a loud scream. Terry had come running downstairs from his bedroom when he heard his sister's scream (he had returned home earlier but had gone straight upstairs to his room without looking into the darkened dining room—porch area). They had then called Meg, who immediately came over to the house, and had called all the local hospitals to see if their mother had been brought in.

When the group returned to the living room, Fred turned on the tape-recorder again and asked Tina for physical descriptions of Teresa and Vince Ferucci. Teresa was of medium height and weight, age forty, with dark hair and large dark eyes, like her daughter's. Vince was about six feet tall and fairly hefty, about two hundred pounds; he had a mustache and thinning hair.

Next, Jo asked Tina about the spots all over the house where black circles had been drawn on the walls. Tina explained that those were the places where the police had found blood smeared on the walls, probably made by Vince as he rushed around trying to change his clothes and get Teresa out to the trunk.

"Tina, are there any construction areas nearby where Vince could have buried the body before a structure was built on top of the site?" Stephen asked.

"As a matter of fact, there was a construction site right on this street—an empty lot with woods right next to it. But the police had already checked out both areas and found nothing."

Stephen conferred with his investigators to see what their next step should be. Fred suggested that Jo try psychometry (a process in which a psychic holds an item and tries to pick up vibrations or information about its owner). When Jo agreed, Meg and Tina took her into Teresa's bedroom and handed her a red-and-white-striped shirt that had been one of Teresa's favorites.

"When was the last time your mother wore this?" Jo asked.

"During that week sometime."

Jo held the shirt and concentrated for a while, but did not get any impressions. Meg and Tina then gave her a bathrobe that Teresa had worn every day, and a tan pants suit. Jo asked Meg and Tina to leave the bedroom now, so that she could be sure the information she picked up wasn't transmitted telepathically from the two women. Jo turned on the tape-recorder as she sat on Teresa's bed, holding the clothing, and recorded the following:

"I get nothing from the bathrobe or the pants outfit. But when I hold the red-and-white-striped polo shirt now, I get a feeling of urgency. I feel very nervous, very uptight and afraid. But I get no clue as to where she is now, except that I feel the location is close."

When Jo returned to the living room, Connie suggested that it might be helpful to see samples of Vince's photography. (Vince was a professional photographer, but he had been unemployed for the last two years.) Tina brought Vince's portfolio into the dining room and spread the photographs out on the table. Stephen and his researchers were stunned. Vince's work was magnificent.

"Art for art's sake," Tina said. "That's my father's law. If he didn't think a job offer was artistic, he wouldn't accept it."

Suddenly the wail of a police siren intruded on the stillness of the night. "Every time I hear that," Tina said quietly, "it makes me nervous."

Fred cleared his throat. "Tina, do you think your mother could still be alive?"

"No, she's definitely dead. He killed her. I think it was premeditated. I don't think he had planned it for

127

that particular night, but I think it's been building up for a long time."

"Meg, what are your feelings?" Fred asked.

"I think Vince murdered her."

"Where were the divorce papers located?" Stephen asked.

"They were at my house," Meg replied. "My husband was Teresa's attorney, and he had brought the papers home with him from the office, all ready for Teresa to sign. Teresa was at my house when my husband got home, but he was exhausted and wanted to nap for a while. So he told Teresa to go home, make dinner, and do whatever else she had to do, and then be back at our house at seven-thirty to go through the papers and sign them. He told her they could get it all out of the way that night and serve the papers on Vince by the next week.

"So Teresa left my house at five o'clock and went home," Meg continued. "She left the papers at our house. When she hadn't come back by seven-thirty, I didn't worry, because she was always about fifteen minutes late. By eight o'clock I was getting nervous, so I started calling here. But Vince never answered. That wasn't unusual for him, because Vince never answered the phone anyway—that was one of his quirks. I thought Teresa was probably taking a shower and that she would be a little later. In the meantime, my husband was getting annoyed that she hadn't arrived, and he finally went to bed, saying that she could sign the papers tomorrow. At about eight-twenty, I drove over here to bring the papers to Teresa. I left my house just a few minutes before eight-thirty, and I'm only three blocks away. I pulled into the driveway behind Vince's car, and my bright lights were on. I saw Vince through the window, getting up from a crouched position on the porch and walking very quickly to the kitchen to shut off the porch light. I thought this a bit odd, since Vince usually moved very slowly.

"You know the rest. When Vince or Teresa didn't answer the door, I started pounding on the door and screaming for them. I figured that Vince was down in the basement, since he had gone in that direction."

"You screamed and pounded on the door because you sensed that something was wrong?" Stephen asked.

"No. I didn't sense anything. I was just annoyed that she was keeping my husband waiting, when he was so tired. I felt she was putting him out, and I was angry! Anyway, then Vince called out and said he wasn't dressed and that Teresa was on her way to my house. If I'd been thinking clearly, I would have realized that her car was still parked in front of the house. But I didn't notice it. I just jumped back into my car, flew back to my house, and ran inside looking for Teresa. But of course she wasn't there. Then Terry called wanting to know where his mother was. I told him that I didn't know."

"Had Terry noticed any signs of violence when he came in?" Stephen asked.

"The porch light was off when he came in," Tina answered, "and the blackboard said 'Mom's at Meg's.' My father usually wrote pretty legibly, but this message was scribbled."

Earl Logan, the friend of the family, who had been quiet until now, said, "Meg, you said you saw him run into the hallway. There are doors leading from there to the bathroom and to the basement. Maybe he hid the body in the basement."

"But it was the porch light that he switched off," Meg said.

"Yes, but he may have done that so you couldn't see all the blood there. Then he could have run to the basement door to 'stand guard,' the way a person normally does when one has something to cover up and doesn't want anyone to come into that area."

Meg shrugged. "The basement was searched— there was no sign of a body down there."

"Tina," Stephen said, "when your mother was leaving the house to go to Meg's, would she have had a pocketbook with her?"

"Yes. As a matter of fact, the police found it in the car. For some reason, he hadn't gotten rid of it. He said that he remembered he still had it in the car when he went to Long Beach after midnight."

"Why would he go to Long Beach?" Stephen was puzzled.

"He said he was going fishing," Tina said slowly. Then she paused. "After finding my mother's bag, he said he put it into a laundry bag in the car; one with the word *laundry* written on it. But we don't have any bags like that. Anyway, he claims he put the pocketbook in the laundry bag and said to himself, 'I have to take it to Tina; I want Tina to have everything in the pocketbook.'

"Then, the second time I saw him in prison, he said, 'I was with Mom all weekend. She was kissing me through a black veil.' But when my aunt questioned him about it, he said he had only meant that he saw her in his mind."

Stephen wondered if it was in Vince's mind or if perhaps he had seen a ghost.

"Of course, it could all have been an act," Tina continued. "My father is usually very precise. If you

130

asked him where the bathroom was, he'd explain the plumbing system. His IQ is supposedly 190."

"He was very introverted, though, wasn't he?" Stephen asked.

"If you mean he didn't have any friends, that's true. He rarely went out. My mother was more extroverted, and she was embarrassed to go out with him."

"What did your mother do for a living?"

"She was a singing teacher and a performer in local stage productions."

At that moment, the other PIA investigators arrived. After introductions were made, Jack looked at Vince's photographs while Sandra studied the letters that Stephen had analyzed, hoping to get impressions of Vince's personality.

Jack, a professional photographer, was impressed with Vince's work. "Very professional and very precise," he concluded. "He really knew what he was doing, really had a feel for his work, a great sense of composition."

Sandra's psychic impressions, gained through study of Vince's letters, matched the observations of both Stephen and the graphologist. "He's schizoid, capable of being very logical. I'm sure he's very intelligent, but I'm also sure he has another facet of his personality that has no mind involved at all. If he did something, this personality would cover up what the other one did." She paused. "My other impression is that if she was trying to leave him, he wouldn't let her go under any conditions."

Everyone was astounded. No one had told Sandra that Teresa had been planning to leave Vince.

The newly arrived investigators were given a summary of the events surrounding Teresa's disappearance. Then Fred took Sandra through all the rooms of the house, as he had done with Jo, and showed her the pieces of Teresa's clothing that Jo had attempted to psychometrize.

Sandra held the clothing but preferred not to tape-record her impressions at that time.

Back in the living room, with the tape-recorder on, the discussion continued.

"Did your father carry any propane lamps or anything like that?" Sandra asked.

"Yes. He had fishing lamps that worked off the battery of his car."

"Could the police tell if the lamps had been used when he got back?"

"I don't think so. They could tell about the gasoline in the car, though. They figured out that he'd used up a little over eleven gallons of gas."

Sandra abruptly changed the subject: "Is it possible that Teresa's body was burned and disposed of?"

"I don't think he would do that to my mother," Tina said. "Besides, all the incinerators in the area have high fences. Wherever she is, she's in one piece, or as close to one piece as possible, I think."

Meg added: "A psychiatrist also said that he didn't think Vince would have mutilated her to that point, because of his feelings for her."

Earlier Stephen had spoken privately with Jo and Sandra about their psychic impressions. After looking at the map of the south shore, Stephen felt very strongly that Teresa's body had been dumped into the ocean. Jo, too, had looked at the map, but she felt that Teresa was hidden on land, perhaps in a county park. Sandy's impressions were far more horrifying; she felt that Teresa had been cut up in pieces, placed in plastic bags, and dumped into an incinerator. She had

had a psychic vision of the incinerating plant: a building located near water, surrounded by a fence that was easy to get past, with the entire area illuminated by pink lights. Stephen thought the pink lights sounded unlikely, but Sandy was insistent on that point.

Stephen told Meg and Tina that he wanted to check out some of the local areas along the south shore. "Both Jo and I had impressions about certain areas on the map," he explained, "though I am more inclined to believe that Teresa is in water, while Jo feels she is buried on land." Stephen paused, trying to think of a delicate way to tell Tina about Sandra's impressions.

Seeming to sense Stephen's dilemma, Sandra looked at Tina with great compassion and said softly, "I think your mother was mutilated . . . chopped up. I don't think you're going to find her."

"You think he had time to do that?" Tina asked, pale.

"I think he made time," Sandra answered.

Sandra then told the group of her impression that Teresa's mutilated remains had been burned beyond recognition in an incinerator somewhere nearby on the south shore. Tina thought that all the incinerators in the area had security guards and were surrounded by very tall fences that would be virtually impossible to scale. Sandra, however, was sure that the fence around this incinerator was either very low or perhaps broken.

It was now past midnight. Stephen told Meg and Tina that he would contact them as soon as he and his team had checked out the previously mentioned areas along the south shore.

Meg and Tina seemed greatly relieved.

One week later, Stephen, Roxanne, Jo, and Connie drove out to the south shore. Their first stop was Point Lookout, a beach and fishing area. They walked along the white sand, enjoying the light breeze, and the late-fall sunshine. They saw nothing out of the ordinary, nor did they experience any psychic impressions.

Their next stop was Cow Meadow Park, an isolated spot on a peninsula stretching out into Middle Bay. The ground was spongy and covered with waist-high marsh grass and other plants. It looked like an ideal place to hide something.

As they walked out to the tip of the peninsula the sky became overcast. There were no other people in sight. They walked with downcast eyes, searching the grass, not knowing what they expected to find.

Stephen walked to the water's edge and stood there watching the tide come in. He had that feeling again. He had never considered himself psychic, but somehow he felt sure that Teresa's body had been dumped into the ocean somewhere along this shoreline.

Jo, Connie, and Roxanne felt that it was a melancholy, barren place, but they did not pick up any psychic impressions.

Next they visited a large town incinerator about five miles from Cow Meadow Park. As they drove up the long driveway, they saw that the plant was surrounded by a heavy chain-link fence about twelve feet high. A security guard stopped them at the gate. Stephen told the guard that they were looking for an incinerator surrounded by a low fence located somewhere near water. The guard directed them to the Freeport incinerator, which matched that description.

The Freeport incinerator was on an old, pitted road, with no driveway leading up to it. There were no security guards in sight. Stephen parked next to the old, rusted, chain-link fence, which was only about six feet high and had a gaping hole where a section had collapsed. On the far side of the low brick building was a man-made canal. The incinerator appeared to be closed, not a soul was in sight. Anyone could walk through the hole in the fence and enter the building, for its bay doors had been left open. Stephen couldn't imagine why the doors had been left open. All that was missing from Sandra's vision were the pink lights.

It was dusk now, and Stephen decided to head home. As he and Jo, Connie, and Roxanne walked back to the car in the fading light, the area was suddenly illuminated by lights around the incinerator building, which had turned on automatically at dusk.

The lights were pink.

The following Saturday night, Stephen, Sandra, Roxanne, Faith, and Connie held a séance at the Ferucci house. They hoped to contact Teresa so that she could tell them where her body could be found. Meg had agreed to attend the séance, but Tina did not wish to.

After Meg and the investigators had taken their seats at the dining-room table, in the center of which Faith had set a candle in a holder, Stephen explained how they would proceed:

"As soon as the lights are turned off and the candle is lit, everyone will join hands on top of the table and concentrate on Teresa. Sandra will attempt to sense psychically whether Teresa is present and whether she can communicate with us. We hope for some physical sign of her presence—some sight or sound to let us know she is here. But this may not happen. It often takes a great deal of time and patience before getting any results in these things, and sometimes we get nothing at all. But we'll try our best."

Meg then turned out the lights, Connie lit the candle, and everyone joined hands. The cassette tape recorder was on, ready to record whatever might happen.

After a few minutes of silence, Stephen said softly, "Teresa, can you make yourself seen or heard, or give us a sign?"

Everyone remained silent, their eyes closed as they concentrated on Teresa.

Five minutes later, Stephen spoke again. "The only impression I'm getting is of a fish hook being dipped into water. Blue water. I also had a brief impression of Teresa in a light brown coat."

Sandra remained motionless in her seat, her eyes closed and her head back. Stephen thought he heard a humming sound in the room, like a boat whistle in the distance. The sound continued for about two minutes. When it stopped, he asked if anyone else had heard anything. Everyone nodded; they, too, had heard it.

Now that they all had their eyes open, Faith pointed out that the candle flame seemed to be growing taller. Stephen had seen this at other séances, but he didn't know if it was a sign of a ghostly presence or if it was caused by the psychic energy generated by the six of them concentrating so intensely. Stephen then said that he had been able to picture the argument between Teresa and Vince but not what had occurred afterward. Roxanne had had an impression of Teresa being hit while standing in the doorway.

Suddenly Sandra spoke, her eyes closed, her voice barely more than a whisper. "She's here. I can feel her. Teresa is here."

"Where is she?" Meg asked.

"She's standing over there, near the door." Everyone looked toward the porch door, but they saw nothing. However, Sandra insisted that Teresa was there.

"My feet are like ice," Meg whispered, and Stephen realized that it had become colder in the room within the last few minutes.

Sandra spoke again. "I'm seeing a front door. It's over to the right of the house. Not this house, but it's a lovely house. . . . Curtains . . . Not a big house . . ."

"I heard the word *Tuesday* in my mind," Stephen said. "What did Teresa do on the Tuesday before she died?"

"She might have had a rehearsal," Meg said.

"Sandra, can you ask Teresa if she's at peace? Does she realize what happened to her?" Stephen asked.

Sandra, her eyes closed as if in a slight trance, said softly, "Yes, she knows. It happened."

"Can you find out from Teresa where her body is located?"

Sandra hesitated for a few minutes before answering. "I almost had a feeling of a body being dragged. Terrible feeling."

Suddenly there was a loud groan.

"What was that?" Connie whispered, frightened.

"Probably just the house settling," Stephen said, though he wasn't at all certain. Everyone was feeling uncomfortable, and it was getting colder by the minute.

"I feel very, very cold," Stephen said, "on my back, too."

"She's here," Sandra said. "Now we just have to communicate."

"I feel nervous," Stephen admitted.

"I'm scared stiff," Roxanne whispered.

"I'm freezing," Meg said.

"Now don't everybody get scared," Sandra said. "We're not going to accomplish anything by getting scared."

Sandra then suggested that Teresa might be able to communicate better through the Ouija board. They had brought one along in case the psychics needed help in receiving messages from Teresa's spirit. The Ouija board consisted of a board with the letters of the alphabet, the numbers 0 through 9, and the words *Yes* and *No*. A small plastic indicator called a planchette was placed on the board in the center; two people would place the fingers of one hand lightly on the planchette, allowing it to move smoothly over the board until the planchette stopped directly over a letter. A third person would record each letter as it was called out; when the planchette stopped, the message would be complete.

The lights would have to be turned on in order for them to use the board, but Stephen was afraid that this might cause Sandra to lose whatever tenuous contact she had with Teresa. However, Sandra assured him that it would be all right. "Teresa is here,

138

and she says she's not going to go away if we put on the lights," she said.

"She's here; I can feel her now," Stephen said suddenly.

Roxanne said that she, too, felt Teresa's presence.

While Connie went to get the Ouija board, Meg pushed up the thermostat and Faith blew out the candle. It was agreed that Meg would take notes while Connie worked the Ouija board with Sandra.

"Now, we're going to try to communicate with you, Teresa," Sandra began. "Please don't go away."

After several minutes, the planchette began to move. It spelled out c-o-l-d.

"It's so cold in here," Roxanne said. "Meg, didn't you put on the heat?"

"I pushed it up fifteen minutes ago. All the other rooms are very warm."

"Is this room normally as warm as the others?" Stephen asked.

"It's normally *warmer* than the others."

Sandra moaned. "My legs . . . They're so cold and numb."

Abruptly, four loud banging sounds seemed to come from the next room. The group looked at one another nervously, as two more bangs sounded. They were louder now, and getting closer. Everyone stared in the direction of the hallway. There was no one else in the house except the six of them in the dining room.

"Isn't that noise coming from the cellar?" Roxanne whispered, voicing what all of them had been afraid to say. Each had been afraid that he was the only one hearing the sounds.

Another bang was heard, apparently coming from the other side of the closed basement door. The sounds, or footsteps, as they seemed to be, had gotten progressively louder and closer to the basement door, as though something was climbing up the stairs. Twelve bangs for twelve steps.

"It sounded like the stairs, something dragged up the steps," Roxanne whispered.

No more footsteps were heard. Reluctantly, Stephen volunteered to go check out the basement.

Connie offered to accompany him. "After all, if it is Teresa, there's nothing to be afraid of, is there?" she said, but she looked uneasy.

Stephen was far more frightened than he had let on. In all his years of investigating supernatural phenomena, he had never heard a physical manifestation as clearly as those footsteps on the stairs.

However, he and Connie found nothing unusual in the basement. When they returned to the dining room a few minutes later, they reported that they had seen nothing that might account for the sounds. Stephen then turned off the tape recorder and rewound the tape. If the footsteps had come out on tape, the investigators would have solid evidence of a paranormal phenomenon. Stephen was confident that the footsteps would come out, for they had been quite loud.

As Stephen pushed the playback button, everyone leaned forward, eager to hear confirmation of the bizarre event they had witnessed.

The tape played. Sandra was heard saying, "*My legs. They're so cold and numb.*" Silence. Everyone waited to hear the footsteps. But there was only the sound of people stirring in their seats, followed by more silence. Then, a few moments later, Roxanne's voice: "*Isn't that noise coming from the cellar?*"

The footsteps should have been picked up between Sandra's and Roxanne's statements. Stephen rewound the tape and played it again. The voices were there, loud and clear, but there were no sounds of footsteps or banging.

They tried the Ouija board again, but without much success. Sandra kept seeing the name *Melanie*. Later, Tina explained that Melanie was a new music student of Teresa's, with whom she had had an appointment on Tuesday. Perhaps that was why Stephen had heard the word *Tuesday* during the séance. The Ouija board gave them no lead on where to find Teresa.

The investigators left the Ferucci house discouraged that they couldn't locate Teresa, but amazed that she had been able to make them physically aware of her presence. They were all certain that the footsteps on the basement steps had been Teresa's despite the fact that the sounds had not been recorded.

After the séance at the Ferucci home in mid-October, the Parapsychology Institute of America tried using other psychics to locate Teresa's body. On Halloween night, Stephen conducted another séance, live on the air, for a local radio talk show, using a psychic whom he had met recently.

The psychic said she had a "feeling of water, possibly the Great South Bay." She also felt that towels had been wrapped around Teresa's face (towels *were* missing from the Ferucci home), and that Teresa had been hit on the ear. (Months later, at Vincent Ferucci's trial, they learned that the clump of skin Tina had found in the dining room was part of Teresa's earlobe.)

141

During most of this on-the-air séance, a high-pitched humming sound was heard by the participants, and by hundreds of listeners, who called in to say that they were hearing a strange hum in the background of the program. The engineers at the station found no logical or technological explanation for the sound. It was very similar to the humming sound heard by the research team during the séance at the Ferucci house, which Stephen had described as being like a distant boat whistle.

This séance, too, failed to turn up Teresa Ferucci's body. However, Vincent Ferucci was convicted of first-degree manslaughter in March 1977, and was sentenced to eight-and-a-half to twenty-five years in prison (though he is up for parole soon and may be freed by the time you read this). During the trial, a fellow inmate of Ferucci's testified that Vincent had admitted to him that he had killed his wife, cut her up, and dumped the pieces into Great South Bay. Teresa's body had still not been found, so Vincent Ferucci became one of the first people to be convicted of manslaughter without a body as evidence.

Three and a half years later, in late November 1980, an off-duty police officer and his wife were walking their dog along an empty beach in Hampton Bays in eastern Suffolk County. The man noticed two shoes sticking out of the sand. He kicked them . . . and found a skeleton attached. It was Teresa Ferucci, still wearing what was left of the clothing and jewelry she'd worn on the day of her murder. She was identified by dental X-rays and by fitting her partial dental plate to the skull of the skeleton. An autopsy showed that she'd suffered severe fracture of the facial bones and a fractured skull.

Hampton Bays is east of the Great South Bay. It

142

is quite possible that the body was carried east by the tides, washed up on shore, and covered by sand. Stephen Kaplan's conviction that Teresa Ferucci was in water had turned out to be correct, as had Sandra Collins's psychic vision of Vincent Ferucci dismembering his wife's body.

In 1983, Roxanne Kaplan played the original séance tape as she prepared to reconstruct this story. She got the shock of her life.

Teresa Ferucci's ghostly footsteps, dragging loudly up the basement stairs, could now be heard clearly and distinctly. . . .

Beware the Man
in Black

It began more than three hundred years ago, with an enormous explosion that caused many deaths. Since then, the deaths have been quieter, but the results have been the same: each has added one more ghost to Beardslee Manor.

This true tale was gathered from many sources, but not from the most likely source. The local library kept a large file on Beardslee Manor, the area's most famous landmark; however, the file has mysteriously disappeared.

Over the past forty-odd years, there have been many auto accidents on Route 5 near the manor. Rather than detail each one, a composite is presented to demonstrate all the bizarre phenomena that have occurred there over the years—and which have frightened motorists out of their wits!

The bloody history of Beardslee Manor is a fascinating one, one that has spilled over into the present. . . .

Beardslee Manor is located just outside the tiny, affluent town of Little Falls, New York, in the historic Mohawk Valley, an area in which many Revolutionary battles were fought. But bizarre happenings at Beardslee Manor began long before the manor was built—and long before the first Beardslee set foot on the land.

In 1750, East Canada Creek, or East Creek as it was called then, held a fort on the site of what is now Beardslee Manor. The French settlers had fought the Indians there. Several years later, the Indians joined forces with the French against the British, who were moving north to attack Canada. The fort was the major supply depot for the British forces in the area.

One night, a war party of seventeen Mohawks moved silently through the moonlit forest toward the fort. The plan had been hatched by their leader, Bear Claw, and a French commandant.

When Bear Claw saw that there were only two redcoats guarding the entrance to the fort, he mimicked a crow's call, which was the signal to begin. Two of the warriors, Running Deer and Little Bear, crept up on the lone British sentries.

Running Deer and Little Bear were sharp and swift with their knives, both guards died quickly and silently.

The braves ran to the now-unguarded doors of the fort and pushed them open. The war party then crept into the fort and pushed the doors closed, so that anyone looking at the entrance would see nothing amiss. Bear Claw had been told by the French commandant that the British weapons cache was in a room at the end of an underground tunnel. Taking a torch from one of the walls to light the way, Bear Claw led his party down the stone corridor.

What Bear Claw had not been told was that the door to the room had a heavy padlock on it. They would have to hack their way through the door and they would have to do it quickly. At midnight, the British watch would change and the dead guards would be discovered.

Just as Little Bear began using his ax on the lock, a small party of British soldiers returned to the fort! The two braves left to guard the entrance let out an anguished wolf howl, the signal that danger was near.

Little Bear and another warrior continued to batter the lock, while Bear Claw leaped up the stairs and led his braves into battle with the British. The hand-to-hand combat was fierce as the English got their first lesson in guerrilla warfare.

In the subterranean stone corridor, Little Bear and his companion finally broke through the door. Then they grinned; the room was filled with barrels of gunpowder. They had never seen so much of the black powder before. In a few moments, the fort would be gone, and maybe, in time, the white men would be gone too.

Little Bear and the other warrior broke open the barrel nearest them. Then, carefully holding the barrel between them so that the gunpowder ran out onto the floor, they began to spread a trail from the center of the room out into the corridor. When the trail was long enough, they would ignite it with their torch. The entire fort would be destroyed in the resulting explosion.

Just as the two warriors reached the corridor, a redcoat ran down the steps, musket at the ready, and saw what they were doing. He fired instantly. A hot lead ball struck Little Bear in the chest, sending him sprawling back and causing the barrel to fall from

146

both warriors' hands. The other Mohawk had also been carrying the torch; now he dropped it, ripped the dagger from his waistband, and launched himself at the redcoat before the soldier could reload his musket. A fierce fight ensued. Neither man noticed that the torch had fallen into the carefully laid trail of gunpowder.

In the middle of their hand-to-hand battle, the young soldier and the determined Mohawk saw a white flash for about an eighth of a second. Then they were both incinerated by the blast.

The fort was ripped apart. In the town, the church shook and the bell rang out in the night. It was a death knell. Nothing was left but ashes. Seventeen braves had died defending their land and people, and the British were gone. But not for long.

A new war would begin, one for independence from England. The area around East Creek and Little Falls would see more bloodshed before the Revolutionary War was won and the first Beardslee would settle in this area.

John Beardslee was born in 1759 in Sharon, Connecticut.

Following the Revolutionary War, having traveled extensively, he found that he was particularly attracted to the Mohawk Valley.

Beardslee was a practical mechanic, an architect, and a civil engineer, so he naturally was of much use in this growing land. In 1792, he built for the state a mill for the use of the Oneida Indians. Between 1790 and 1796 he built the first bridge across the Mohawk River at Little Falls and the old red grist mill there; he also built mills at Van Hornesville and the courthouse and jail at Herkimer.

Tall, rugged, John Beardslee was an individualist

who loved hunting and fishing; he loved the virgin land around East Creek. In 1794 he selected a hundred-acre lot as his estate. By 1795, the grist mills that Beardslee had built were in operation, and soon the community flourished. People flocked to the area known as The City or Beardslee's City and settled there. Eventually it boasted mills, two stores, two taverns, a blacksmithing shop, a nail factory, a brewery, a distillery, a lead and silver mine—the only silver mine in the state, in fact—a doctor, a lawyer, traveling entertainment, and turkey shoots.

Beardslee's City was a boom town. But, like the boom towns of the California gold rush some years later, the boom turned to bust.

Factors such as the movement west and the construction of the Erie Canal and the Mohawk highway drew away the residents. Eventually, Beardslee's City became a ghost town. Today, all traces of the town have disappeared, except for a few gravestones, which have been vandalized.

Augustus Beardslee was born on August 13, 1801. After the death of his father in 1825, Augustus inherited the estate, which by then had increased by three hundred acres. John Beardslee had built up and helped civilize the area. Now it was up to his son, Augustus, to continue the tradition.

Around 1860, after years of serving as a county judge, Augustus began construction of Beardslee Manor, near what is now Route 5, on the site of the former fort where so many had died. It took several years for George W. Heller, the builder, to complete the extraordinary mansion.

The hand-cut gray stone building, modeled after an old castle in Ireland, was three stories high, with the second and third floors containing bedrooms with adjoining baths and music and study rooms. Augustus spared no expense in furnishing the manor. Furniture and paintings were imported from the best estates in Europe; rugs came from the Middle East and the Orient. The decor was an overwhelming mixture of styles and textures unlike anything the townspeople had ever seen before. Despite the mile-long stone wall that surrounded the isolated manor, Augustus always welcomed visitors, not only to see its interior but to enjoy the Beardslee hospitality.

Augustus's young son, Guy Roosevelt, was so impressed by the manor that he wanted someday to build something of his own. Like his grandfather, John, Guy was both ambitious and adventurous. As a young man, he attended West Point, from which he was graduated in 1879. He was then sent West to fight in the Indian wars.

He returned to East Creek a few years later. Augustus had died and the manor was now Guy's. He was determined to build up the farm and to pursue new interests, such as railroads, dams, and Thomas Edison's recent discovery—electricity. . . .

From 1750, when the fort was destroyed, to the time Guy Roosevelt Beardslee became interested in electricity, there were no reports of supernatural phenomena on the site. But now things began to change.

In 1892, Beardslee, with two engineers and a lawyer from New York City, began a project to develop water power at East Canada Creek about a mile from the manor. He planned to use water power to generate electricity not only for the manor but for the whole town of Saint Johnsville.

However, Guy found that no one wanted to invest in his project. The development of water power was old hat, but to use water power to generate electricity and then to send that electricity over the tremendous distance of three miles seemed too risky.

But Guy did not despair. Encouraged by his new wife, Ethel Shriver, whom he had married in 1895, Guy abandoned his attempts to get financial backing and decided to build a hydroelectric station himself. He purchased two revolving-armature generators from a piano manufacturer in Saint Johnsville and began construction of a power station. He also entered into a contract with the village to provide streetlights.

One of the workers on the hydroelectric station was Domini Jake, an old acquaintance. He was one of the few people who knew that Beardslee Manor contained underground tunnels and secret passageways. In fact, one of the tunnels, which ran from the basement up to a hill, was the stone corridor of the original fort. Everyone knew the terrible story; hence, the end of the tunnel was known as Indian Hill.

One day Domini Jake went into one of the passageways. Perhaps he planned to steal some of the immensely valuable artifacts in the Beardslee home. Perhaps he was searching for an archaeological find related to the old fort. Perhaps he had seen or heard something. We'll never know. Other laborers found Domini Jake hanged in one of the underground tunnels. He had been there for some time. No one knew why he had killed himself, but he was dressed in black, as if for his own funeral. . . .

Jake's death did not delay Guy Beardslee's work. Electricity was brought to the manor. The wiring was installed by John D. Cairns—a job well done, as evidenced by the fact that the original wiring is still in use today.

Beware the Man in Black

On Saint Patrick's day, 1898, Guy Beardslee's generators illuminated the streets of Saint Johnsville. The future of the little town was assured. The townspeople celebrated. Saint Johnsville would soon become a hub of industry. Guy Beardslee, whose wild ideas had been scorned, had been proved right.

Guy soon became a rich man, or rather a richer one. Farms and mills all over the county began purchasing electricity from him. With his newfound wealth, he built a railroad siding near the manor. Any train passing could be signaled and stopped at his private Beardslee Station.

Guy now had everything he had ever wanted: his home, his wife, and his son, Guy, Jr. It was this son who would continue in the Beardslee tradition, who would inherit the vast estate. Guy Beardslee could not have known that fate had something else in store.

One summer afternoon, as Guy was tending his beloved gardens, he felt a sudden chill in the air, as though a cloud had passed in front of the sun, although none had. He shivered, glanced about, and realized that he was not alone.

He saw one of his handymen on a horse. There was something else on the horse, something small and very still. . . .

Guy cried out in anguish. His son, Guy, Jr., had drowned in the creek.

Guy Beardslee, Jr., was buried in the family mausoleum on the grounds of the estate. After that, Guy, Sr., lost all interest in his work. He retired from the East Creek Electric Light and Power Company in 1912, and devoted himself to raising his prize dairy stock.

Then disaster struck again, in February 1919. The fire seemed to have started in one of the main rooms. The flames spread quickly, destroying the huge paintings and antique furnishings.

Fortunately, Ethel Beardslee was a light sleeper. When she awoke she thought she had heard a voice, quite similar to her dead son's, telling her to get out of the room quickly.

Ethel jumped out of bed, opened the door, and saw the fast-rising flames. She woke Guy, and together they left the building via one of the many secret passageways. Supposedly built in case of Indian attack, these passageways were concealed behind three feet of stone. No flames could penetrate them.

Guy and Ethel, in their bedclothes, stood helpless in the cold night air and watched as the manor went up in flames. The family history, three generations' worth of heirlooms, all gone in seconds.

The following morning, however, when Guy discovered the real extent of the damage, he was even more devastated. Not only had the fire almost totally demolished his home, it had killed a large number of his prize dairy stock.

No amount of money could replace the furnishings that Augustus Beardslee had imported more than sixty years before. The best Guy could do was construct a flat roof over the first floor of his castle. He then began the arduous task of replacing his dairy stock. The cost was astronomical; it nearly depleted the family savings.

About a year later, when the house had been restored as much as possible, Guy resumed his favorite hobby: electricity. He was fascinated when he learned of the bizarre experiments being conducted by Thomas Edison and a scientist named Nikola Tesla. Tesla believed that electrical charges were present in the human body and that those charges might continue after death. Edison, combining Tesla's theories with his own practical know-how, was now trying to construct a machine to talk to the dead.

Guy was intrigued.

Even before the fire, although Guy could not pinpoint the exact time, he and various workers at the manor had seen strange things—indistinct figures in the darkness that would disappear when they went to investigate. Sometimes Guy had wondered if it might be the ghosts of the British and Indians killed at the fort, or perhaps the ghost of Domini Jake. But now, in a flash of hope, he wondered if it might be Guy, Jr.

Reading all he could find in the scientific journals, Guy decided to follow in Edison's footsteps; Guy, too, would construct a machine to talk to the dead. Soon the nights were split by blue-white arcs of electricity as Guy proceeded with his experiments. This bluish glow would figure prominently in the many horrors to come, after yet another mysterious death.

The Beardslees had a trusted and reliable handyman who retrieved the daily mail. At that time, the manor still had the private railroad station, and it was there that their mail was delivered. Every day the handyman would walk along the railroad tracks to the station, pick up the mail, and bring it back to the manor without delay. But then one day the handyman didn't return from the mail pickup.

Thinking he might somehow have been hurt, Guy sent out another worker to search for him. To the second man's horror, he found part of a body near the railroad tracks. The head had been ripped off.

Sickened by the grisly find, the worker returned to the manor and reported what he'd seen. Guy accompanied the man back to the tracks and was shocked by the horrible sight. It looked as though the head had been ripped off by the force of an oncoming train and the body dragged perhaps a quarter of a mile. Pieces of flesh and pools of blood covered the ground. But the handyman's head was nowhere to be found.

How had such a gruesome death occurred? The handyman had made the pickup every day for years. It was always evident when a train was coming; it blew its whistle. Guy had no explanation.

The next death on the estate was Guy's; he died on January 15, 1939.

But did Guy really leave after he died? Ethel Beardslee and some of the workers kept seeing things . . . not only the dark, ghostly figures of the past, but voices, a swirling mist, and an unaccountable blue light.

There were forces at work within the house. Without Guy, there was nothing to hold Ethel at the manor. First she sold the farm, leaving the house and thirty wooded acres. Then, in 1941, Ethel sold the house and remaining acreage to Mr. and Mrs. A. M. Christensen, who loved the manor and promised to treat it with respect.

Three years after buying Beardslee Manor, the Christensens, faced with mounting expenses, decided to turn the place into a restaurant. It was a chance for the public to enjoy not only the expertly crafted stone mansion but the enchanting grounds and gardens. It was also a chance for the public to become better acquainted with the not-so-human inhabitants as the stories about Beardslee Manor grew. . . .

* * *

Beware the Man in Black

Barry and Enid Miller had nearly completed their long drive from Niagara Falls, where they had spent their honeymoon, to their home in Saint Johnsville. It had been raining lightly throughout the trip. Now, on Route 5, a fog crept up.

Barry turned on his bright headlights, but it didn't help. Suddenly, the fog completely obscured the road ahead. Then the engine coughed and died and Barry's car glided to a halt.

Barry had no idea what was wrong with his car. He had checked it before making the trip and everything had been fine. He tried the various knobs on the dashboard and turned the ignition key several times, but nothing happened. Fortunately, however, the headlights still worked; passing cars would be able to see them, so they would not be hit.

Barry knew he would have to go for help. It was late and nothing would be open, but he thought perhaps he could find a house nearby and phone for assistance. He told Enid to stay in the car, with the doors locked, and not to get out of the car for any reason. He had heard of strange things happening on this stretch of road, ghost stories and such, and he didn't want his new bride to take any chances.

Frightened, Enid stared out the car window as Barry disappeared into the foggy night.

Barry thought the fog seemed to be thinning; he could see trees on both sides of the road. Remembering the direction of some nearby houses, he decided to head through the woods rather than walk miles in the fog and risk being hit by a car. Surely the woods were safer. He was certain he'd be able to see the dim shape of a house through the mist.

Slowly and carefully, he picked his way through the trees; unfortunately, his flashlight was of little help. Suddenly he tripped over a stone wall and fell. When he got back on his feet, he looked around and saw what he thought was a bluish light moving as though someone was carrying a lantern. Hastily, he set out after it.

As Barry drew near the light, he was sure he saw a dim figure moving ahead of him. The figure was dark, and he couldn't tell if it was a man or a woman.

"Wait!" he called. "I need your help!"

The figure slowed and Barry closed the distance between them. Now he could see that it was a man dressed entirely in dark clothing and carrying a lantern that gave off a blue-white light. The man turned and waited as Barry stumbled toward him.

"Am I glad to find you," Barry said to the man. "My car engine stopped and I had to leave my wife alone and I got lost in the woods and—"

Suddenly Barry stopped. The man had not said a word during this time, nor had he changed expression in any way. Puzzled, Barry asked, "Am I disturbing you? I'm sorry, but I need help."

When the man still didn't answer, Barry got angry. "Look, I said I need help!" To emphasize his words, Barry tapped the man on the shoulder with his flashlight.

The flashlight—and Barry's fist—passed right through the man's body.

Barry gasped and stepped back—and the man and the lantern faded from view, leaving only a blue-white light bobbing in the air. Barry turned and ran. . . .

Back on Route 5, Enid sat shivering in the locked car. Fortunately, the fog was lifting and she could see more of the road and the trees surrounding her. In the near distance was a long stone wall, which she recognized as the boundary of Beardslee Manor.

Then, in the far distance, among the trees beyond the stone wall, Enid saw a light moving along as though someone was carrying a lantern or a flashlight. She was sure it was Barry. But as she watched the light, it moved about in the woods without getting any closer. The light looked bluish, which seemed a strange shade for a flashlight.

Just then the fog closed in again; it rolled down the road, obscuring Enid's vision and surrounding the bobbing light. She began blowing the car horn to signal Barry, thinking he must have lost his way. The blue light then changed direction and came toward her.

But the fog quickly closed in once more. Suddenly the white mist swirled around the car and the horn stopped working. However, the light bobbed nearer, and she saw a dark figure. Relief flooded through her; Barry had found her after all.

Suddenly the dark figure disappeared. The ominous fog swirled thicker and faster about the car—and then it coalesced into a horrible face peering in at her through the window. A foul odor permeated the car, and an arcing blue light, like electricity, crackled through the fog. For a breathless moment Enid was stunned into silence. Then she began to scream. . . .

Barry, still stumbling through the woods, heard her. He quickened his pace, but the thick fog confused him. He hurried toward what he thought was the sound and was startled to see a small building loom up in the mist.

He reached out and touched the cold surface. Stone. He shone his flashlight on the front of the building. On the door, a single chiseled word stood out in sharp relief: BEARDSLEE.

To his horror, Barry realized he'd stumbled on to the family mausoleum. Shocked, he dropped the flashlight. Then he dropped to his knees and began frantically searching for it as the night closed in around him and the fog took on an eerie glow. Suddenly he saw a glint of metal. As he reached out toward it, an unseen force pushed him back. He tried to get up, but it was as if two immense arms were pushing him into the wet, cold earth. Terrified, Barry screamed . . . and suddenly, as if the scream somehow released him, the pressure faded and the mist receded. All he could hear now were crickets and Enid's crying.

He snatched up the flashlight and ran to his car. To his amazement, the engine started immediately. And the fog was gone.

Barry and Enid Miller made it out alive; others were not as fortunate. Several people who had automobile accidents near the manor blamed them on mysterious lights; others saw strange lights radiating from behind the manor after their cars had become disabled. But the ghost stories were not confined to passing motorists.

After the death of Pop Christensen in 1956, Beardslee Manor was sold to a man who operated it for the next twenty years. He is convinced that there is something supernatural at the manor, but he's not sure of exactly what it is.

"I can tell you one thing," he said. "In all those years I was there, I never went down into the cellar alone. It was scary as hell."

He explained that many strange things had happened in the cellar: boxes in storage would move by

158

themselves or fall for no reason; he heard strange sounds and sometimes saw an unexplained mist drifting across the floor; lights would turn themselves on and off.

When he sold Beardslee Manor, the new owner took over the restaurant and turned the cellar into a bar. Its unseen inhabitants apparently were not pleased—nor were the bartenders.

The bartenders saw floating balls of blue light, heard loud, heavy breathing coming out of thin air, and saw glasses fall off shelves, pushed by unseen hands. The assistant manager heard voices and screams, saw lights turn off and on, and saw misty apparitions.

But it was not until February 1983 that newspapers and psychic investigators around the country became interested.

The assistant manager had closed for the night. He decided to make a phone call before leaving and went toward the phone. Suddenly, the atmosphere around him turned cold, and the dining-room lights went out. Then something hit him in the chest and sent him reeling. His knees buckled and he fell to the floor. Terrified, he got to his feet and fled for his life.

At about the same time, the manager and other employees distinctly saw an apparition of a man in black. The clothing indicated that the spirit was from the late 1800s. Each time the ghost was spotted, it would disappear immediately.

By April, it was obvious that something had to be done. Norm Gauthier, founder and director of the Society for Psychic Research for New Hampshire, was called in to investigate.

In explaining the existence of ghosts, Gauthier's reasoning was eerily reminiscent of the theories of

Nikola Tesla, which Guy Beardslee had whole-heartedly embraced:

"All of us have an energy field within us. . . . Ghosts are energy forces left behind. The main reason for a ghost's existence is a traumatic or violent death. The spirit stays behind to continue doing what it did when it was incarnated in a body, replaying the death scene, perhaps in a robotic way, or resolving some conflict left at the time of death.

"We live in a four-dimensional world of height, width, depth, and time, but ghosts live in the fifth dimension. The common denominator between us is that our energy forces may be attuned to each other's."

Before beginning his investigation of Beardslee Manor, Gauthier held a press conference in Little Falls. Gauthier had investigated approximately 130 haunted buildings and in some of them had captured strange sounds on tape.

At the press conference, Gauthier announced that he would hold a recording session at Beardslee Manor that night. No daytime noises would disturb or confuse him and his research staff; the spirits would have their time to speak.

"We are born with five senses during the day but we are more open to a sixth sense at night," Gauthier explained. "It is then that we can hear the voices, see the apparitions. . . ."

Gauthier had already set up recording equipment at the manor; microphones had been placed in various "sensitive" areas of the building, where ghosts had reportedly been seen.

That night, at midnight, the ghost-hunting session began.

The lights were dimmed; this would make the spirits feel welcome and not threatened.

Incense was lit. A Bible was opened and placed near several microphones. This was done to ensure that only friendly ghosts would be attracted; the Bible would keep away any more evil entities.

Unfortunately, what was intended as a serious scientific study turned into a media circus. Newspaper, radio, and television reporters had been invited to cover the event. Like locusts, the press descended on Beardslee Manor with their cameras, lights, microphones, and crews.

While in one room Norm Gauthier was trying, without success, to achieve total silence, in another room a television news crew was photographing the local anchorwoman coming down a flight of stairs; she was dressed in period costume and carrying a lit candelabra for atmosphere. Meanwhile, a crew from *PM Magazine* was filming everything, hoping to catch a glimpse of a ghost. It would be great for the ratings. . . .

There was approximately thirty people milling about, hoping to see a ghost. Any sensible spirit would have stayed away. . . .

Norm Gauthier did the best he could. He held four recording sessions, at one-hour intervals, for a total of thirty-five minutes of tape. During the breaks, refreshments were sold in the main hall; one of the more popular drinks was dubbed the Ghost Chaser.

After several hours of "ghost busting," most of the news teams departed. But Joe Kelly, a reporter from the *Utica Observer-Dispatch*, remained. Gauthier told him that he had recorded sounds from the dead before and was convinced that he would get something that night at the manor.

"There are spirits in this building; it is definitely haunted," Gauthier said. "What I'm looking for is a tiny whispered voice. That's the way most of them come over."

Gauthier then pulled out a fresh tape, turned on the recorder, and taped for about eight minutes.

Meanwhile, in another room, some of the employees who had stayed on for the session told their stories.

One waitress reported seeing a man in black in the dining room. He was about six feet tall and dressed in a long black coat and pitch-black pants, both in the style of the late 1800s. Once seen, the figure immediately disappeared.

An inn employee told of being hit in the arms, legs, and chest by an unseen force. He said it had felt like he was being hit by a baseball bat. Although he hadn't been injured by these ghostly blows, he had decided to "get the hell out of there."

Finally, as the sun came up, the remaining reporters packed up their equipment and their valuable tapes . . . valuable because the tapes contained recorded sounds of the ghosts of Beardslee Manor.

The next day, Gauthier and Margie Bilby, a reporter for a local radio station, were shocked. In reviewing their tapes separately, they *both* had recorded something.

Later, Gauthier described the recordings at a press conference in Saint Johnsville:

"During the first session, I recorded a mysterious male voice whispering, 'Who's this person?' This voice was not heard by anyone present during the taping and was not heard by anyone until the tape was played back."

Even more amazing was the tape recorded by

162

Margie Bilby, Gauthier said. "She recorded a ghostly male voice whispering, 'He shoulda got something.' Later, Bilby picked up a female voice whispering, 'Missed you,' followed by a male voice that said, 'Sure have!'"

Margie Bilby herself confirmed this: "Incredibly, my tape-recorder picked up the voices of three ghosts—two men and a woman."

According to Norm Gauthier, ghosts remain on earth because they suffered particularly violent deaths. There have been many violent, strange deaths in and around Beardslee Manor—the Indian band and the British soldiers killed in the explosion of the fort; more deaths during the Revolutionary War; the suicides of Domini Jake and Pop Christensen; the drowning of Guy Beardslee's young son; and the death of Guy himself. . . .

The restaurant at Beardslee Manor is still open to the public. Guests swear they have taken party photos there, only to have a mysterious "mist" outside the windows show up in their pictures. Employees don't like to be in the manor alone when the lights are dim.

Still, having dinner in a haunted house can be appealing. At Beardslee Manor you can combine ghost-hunting with a good meal. But you'll have to drive there, since the train no longer stops there. And you'll have to drive down Route 5, which still provides the townspeople with ghost stories. You shouldn't have any trouble locating the manor; take exit 29A off the New York State Thruway, then head east on Route 5 toward East Canada Creek. But if you see a sudden fog and a dark figure holding a blue lantern, don't get out of your car. . . .

ABOUT SHARON JARVIS

SHARON JARVIS has been a reporter, a teacher, and a tracer of missing persons. For the last sixteen years she has been associated with book publishing, primarily as an editor specializing in science fiction, fantasy, horror, and the occult. Currently she is a literary agent, operating out of a turn-of-the century, ramshackle house on Staten Island, which friends swear must be haunted . . . .

The terrifying new bestseller
by the author of
NATHANIEL and SUFFER THE CHILDREN

JOHN SAUL
BRAINCHILD

La Paloma—once home to a proud Spanish heritage, now a thriving modern community high in the California hills.

And home to a boy named Alex Lonsdale . . . who is about to become the instrument of a terrible, undying evil. An evil that cries out for vengeance for a terrible deed done long ago.

An evil that now waits in the dark and secret places of La Paloma . . . for Alex Lonsdale.

Don't miss John Saul's BRAINCHILD, coming in August 1985 from Bantam Books.